Talk To Me

Workplace Conversations That Work

Sue Johnston

Portfolio
Publishing

Waterloo, Ontario, Canada

Talk To Me
Workplace Conversations That Work
Sue Johnston
Copyright 2012 Sue Johnston

ISBN-13 978-0-9782830-0-1 PRINT
ISBN-13 978-0-9782830-1-8 DIGITAL (.PDF)
ISBN-13 978-0-9782830-2-5 DIGITAL (.EPUB)

Book design by Jim Bisakowski - BookDesign.ca
Editing by Martha Muzychka
Cover illustration by Sue Johnston
Interior illustrations/doodles by Sue Johnston (except where noted)
Appendix Three illustrations copyright iStockphoto.com/MirekP
Author photo by Picture Yourself

First Edition: (May 2012)
10 9 8 7 6 5 4 3 2 1
Published by Portfolio Publishing, Waterloo
It's Understood Communication, Ltd.
505 Forestlawn Road, Waterloo, Ontario, Canada N2K 3Y1
Visit our web site at http://itsunderstood.com

This is a work of fiction. Names, characters, organizations, places and incidents are the product of the author's imagination or are used fictitiously. Any resemblance to people, companies and events in real life is unintended and coincidental.

Web sites referred to in citations and sources of further information may have changed or been removed between the time this book was written (2012) and when it is read.

———•◦•———

Dedicated to the memory of
Linda George
An excellent communicator
And a great friend

———•◦•———

Contents

Acknowledgments

The goal of this book is to help you create connection and collaboration. Those were two of the ingredients in its creation. Though the words are mine, a book such as this is never the work of one person. A host of others provided inspiration, ideas and an occasional push.

I'm fortunate to have had several inspiring managers who are great communicators. They created work environments that let me grow and thrive and supported and coached me when I had lots to learn. Reid Brownscombe, Brian 'B.J.' King, Penny Somerville, Jan McMillan and Trina McQueen stand out. Colleagues, clients and friends provided inspiration as they worked to become better communicators.

Authors and thinkers, such as David Rock, Daniel Goleman, Susan Scott, Dan Pink and Marshall Goldsmith, helped shift my focus from the formal communication that takes place in organizations to the informal communication that takes place between people. By inviting me to speak about face-to-face communication at their events, the International Association of Business Communicators (IABC), Ragan Communications, the Bermuda Bar Association, ASTD Global Network and others helped me refine my ideas. So did my clients in financial services and technology.

Though gone now, my parents continue to shape my views. Al Johnston could engage anyone in conversation and taught me you can learn something from everyone you meet if you ask questions and listen. Helen 'Rick' Johnston provided evidence that you're never too old to learn. They gave me the gene for optimism, a valuable trait in undertaking a project such as this.

Kimberley Robinson, Kathy Gulrich, Susan Meyer and Kay Malone, excellent coaches and friends, helped me start writing and keep writing when it seemed like a crazy idea. Their support and gentle nudging are deeply appreciated. Novelist and teacher Barbara Kyle provided inspiration in her classes and valuable input after my first draft. Author and web pioneer Debbie Weil provided the impetus and support to publish. Friend and fellow corporate communicator Martha Muzychka brought thoughtful editing skills to the project. Jim Bisakowski of bookdesign.ca brought a nice, light touch to the book design. Thanks to all.

I especially thank Andrew Annett, my amazing husband, whose confidence in me is boundless, whose feedback is always truthful and valuable, and without whom none of this would have been possible.

Introduction

The noblest pleasure is the joy of understanding.
– Leonardo da Vinci

Talk To Me: Workplace Conversations That Work is the result of observing a lot of people – myself included – struggle to understand and be understood.

I've had an opportunity to participate in thousands of workplace conversations – first, as a journalist, later as a specialist in organizational communication, and recently as a coach. My interest in how we talk to each other is both professional and personal. It surprises me how little attention organizations give to face-to-face communication.

In the mid-'00s, in conference sessions and journal articles, I began predicting that human conversation would be the next big trend in organizational communication.

I was wrong.

While I was exclaiming, to anyone who would listen, that conversation is the most powerful business tool we will ever have, online social networking was gathering momentum and becoming an unstoppable force. Its novel communication technology looked much more exciting than the hardware and software that comes with human DNA. Organizational communicators turned their attention to platforms and security policies, the ethics of ghostwriting the CEO's blog, and how to capture important ideas in 140 characters.

Conversation didn't turn out to be the next hot communication trend. That's a good thing. Trends come and go. Conversation can – and must – become an enduring process that organizations take seriously and use effectively.

Talk To Me: Workplace Conversations That Work is written to help make that so.

The book introduces concepts of conversation by telling a story. Each chapter contains three sections:

- **Paul's Adventure** – A story in which we witness a fictional manager learn to communicate effectively to salvage a project that's heading for trouble. It illustrates the principles.
- **What's Going On Here?** – A look at management theory or scientific research that explains the situation or supports the approach our hero learns. It illuminates the principles.
- **Do Try This At Home** – A workbook section that offers you points to ponder, exercises to try, and ideas to explore in your own conversations. It invites you to practice.

My goal in sharing this work is to provide readers with a practical understanding of concepts I've learned through study, reading, and personal experience of what has worked for me and my clients. It aims to give you a taste of some interesting ideas and I hope it creates an appetite to learn more.

And as we learn more, we can improve our world, one conversation at a time.

CHAPTER

1

An Invitation to Talk

"Hunchak here," Paul said, faking some energy. Paul Hunchak was not in the mood for another interruption. But he wasn't the sort who could ignore a ringing telephone, even at 6:15 p.m. "No Burt, that's OK." He was lying. He opened a file on his laptop. "Yeah, I got your email about that. The info is all in my report. You know we can't do a thing until Taylor's group gets finished." He rolled his eyes and lip-synched to his caller's words: "This project is mission-critical, mission-critical." More like missing and critical. "Trust me, if anything changes, you'll be the first to know."

Another afternoon had vanished with little evidence that he'd even been at work. And yet, he'd seemed so busy. Burt Shepler's call, quite unnecessary, had been the latest in a series of distractions that had drawn him away from his real work. Whatever that was. It seemed so long since he'd done it.

His official title was Manager, Technology Integration. His elevator speech went something like this: "My team makes sure any new computer systems play nicely with others and that fixing something doesn't break something else." He'd joined Forthright Financial, a specialized wealth management firm, 10 years earlier, when it was a local insurance agency. Today, it had 25,000 employees and 43 offices across the country. As the company grew, his understanding of computers and their applications grew more valuable to Forthright and more interesting to Paul than his understanding of accounting principles. His career had shifted accordingly.

He had five employees reporting to him. They were young, smart, somewhat ambitious, and most of the time, good at their work. They were probably capable of more than they were delivering. But who wasn't? Do people ever live up to their potential? It bothered him that sometimes he had to repeat instructions several times before they got the message. What did he have to do to make them understand? They just didn't get it. Did they believe the same was true of him?

Maybe he just wasn't cut out to manage people. He was afraid to be seen as micromanaging. His own experience with a controlling boss, back in his accounting days, had been de-motivating, demoralizing, and depressing. As a result, almost every serious conversation Paul had with his employees worried him before, during, and after. He was only asking them to do their jobs. Why were they so defensive? Why was he? Were all employees high maintenance nowadays? At least they made up for it by meeting their targets.

The same could not be said for Project Delta. It was two months behind schedule and stumbling towards further delay. Big project. Big team. Big problems. Not quite off the rails, it was barely connecting with them. Paul's formal role, a minor one, was to advise on the technical aspects of merging the new system with other technology developments. It seemed his real role, though unofficial, was referee. It was one that made him feel uncomfortable, ill prepared, and often annoyed.

He wasn't a people person. Not that he was a hermit. He could be highly sociable when it was necessary or when the spirit moved him. He just preferred dealing with things and ideas more than dealing with people. He loved solving the puzzles involved in making things work. It's what had drawn him to jobs in technology. He liked things and situations to be orderly, predictable and working, or if not working, fixable.

This Delta team, if you could call it a team, was neither orderly nor predictable. It sure wasn't working and Paul wasn't certain it could be fixed. He'd witnessed more setbacks on this project than he'd seen in all his years at Forthright. Even at Denman's, the big accounting firm where he'd worked before, things never seemed so grim.

In Paul's mind, two issues conspired to impede progress. The first was that the team held the same conversation at every meeting. It involved the discovery, details and duration of the delay, and it assigned blame. The second was that, despite all the talk, nobody knew what to do. Lately, nobody seemed to care. They had already missed the original target date and were seriously over budget.

The project manager was Burt Shepler. Hired several months earlier to run Project Delta, he looked great on paper. He'd done similar work at a big international bank and had worked with the system vendor before that. He had undoubted technical skills. Unfortunately, he didn't have much else. Worse, he didn't understand Forthright Financial.

Forthright people considered themselves mavericks in the financial services industry. Paul suspected the maverick reputation had more to do with the company's Gold Rush origins and its eccentric founder, Sir Harald Halliday, than with anyone still alive. Yet the pioneering image persisted, and Forthright people enjoyed the notion they were pushing back the industry frontiers.

Burt didn't see how deeply that spirit of independence ran at Forthright. He'd spent most of his 30-year career in one of the world's largest banks. As far as Paul knew, these organizations succeeded through size alone. Using consistent processes over big systems with minimal deviation was the key. He didn't believe *maverick* was a word in the vocabulary of these giant banks, though there might be a truckload of words meaning *consistency, conformity, and compliance.*

Burt ran projects according to his own methodology. Meetings were highly formatted affairs consisting of reports enhanced by yawn-inspiring slideshows. They seemed designed to avoid real dialogue. Burt's assistant, Tara O'Sullivan, keeper of the project plan, presented the weekly update showing the widening gap between targets and reality.

This would be followed by an impassioned speech by Lynnette Benson, from Marketing, about how the folks on the front lines absolutely needed the system and were looking forward to using it and *"could we puhleeeease have a firm date for implementation?"*

Next, Taylor Flynn, who managed the burgeoning group of programmers, would complain about the technical challenges and risks necessitated by Forthright's decision to adapt a vendor's system rather than custombuild one. Then he would go on to describe the week's progress in such detail that even Burt's eyes glazed over.

People responsible for testing, training, documentation, and other Phase Two activities waited. Then they waited some more. Occasionally, they whined, "We can't do a thing without the code." Couldn't they hear themselves? It was the same old whining every week. Paul could handle it for about three minutes. Then, he'd mutter something that questioned whether the conversation was adding value and didn't they have better things to do, such as build a system.

His "mutterances," as his wife, Jenny, liked to call them, shut down more than the complaining. They often brought the meeting to a screeching halt. Most participants considered this a good thing as, by then, it was usually 40 minutes past the notional end time. It never occurred to Paul that someone might be thinking: "Can't he hear himself? It's the same old whining every week."

Why not? It *was* the same meeting every week. Now and then, Burt gave what he considered a motivational speech. The words were a variation of *"Keep up the good work."* The underlying message was *"Make this work or heads will roll."* But it was not motivating Paul. It was not motivating anyone.

Paul had promised to get back to Burt in the morning. As he leafed through the scribbles from the last meeting, he noticed his margin doodles

TALK TO ME

had grown strangely detailed and fantastic. The menacing alien he had drawn was almost a perfect caricature of Burt. And what were the handcuffs about?

He shut the file, shook his head, and closed his eyes.

A third thing on his mind was that, in two weeks, he would turn 45. It was the age at which his father had died. Hard working and hard living, the man had been a heart attack waiting to happen. So it did. Paul had structured his life to be different from his father's, taking care of himself and doing things in moderation. Still, he'd begun to see his dad's face in the mirror each morning and it disturbed him. It reminded him that life is full of uncertainty and things are not always what they seem. He tried to put such thoughts out of his mind. He wasn't like his father. Besides, he had neither the interest in nor the time for a midlife crisis or whatever this might be. He had too much to do.

He surveyed his screen of new emails and the pile of files on his desk and drew a deep breath. He needed to get out and clear his head. Then he'd work late, again, and reduce the pile to a manageable size. There was nothing going on at home – or nothing that he knew about.

As he was about to call Jenny to say he'd be late, the phone rang. What now?

"Hi Paul. It's Emma Bateman." He sensed urgency in the CEO's voice. Why, in heaven's name, was she calling?

"Hello Emma. What can I do for you?"

"Is there a chance you can swing by my office tomorrow afternoon? Maybe around 4:00 or 4:30? I've got a problem, and I'm hoping you'll work with me on it."

What's Going On Here ?

Forthright Financial is not unique. I'll bet you noticed that. Wherever there are people, you can almost guarantee there will be challenges. How we deal with them, as organizations and as individuals, determines our success in getting things done. As work becomes increasingly collaborative, we depend on dozens of other people, inside and outside our organizations, in the next cubicle or five time zones away.

How we work together drives our success. And to work together, we need to talk. The word *conversation* has its roots in Latin and came to English via French. Its literal meaning is *turn with* – *con* (with) and *versare* (turn). The term originally referred to how one operated with others in the world. Long before the 16th century, when it began to refer to talking, the term described relationships. [1]

Real human conversation is the most powerful tool we have at our disposal. It's our organizational operating system. Unlike our tech-enabled business tools, conversation is available regardless of the budget, independent of corporate strategy, and without an Internet connection.

Unfortunately, it's not an intuitive system. And there's no online help.

If comparing workplace conversation with business technology seems odd, think about this. Computer programmers write in code, expressing themselves in programming languages that have very precise syntax, rules, and words. In human conversation, the code consists of words, tone, and body language. In life, as in your laptop, the code prompts a response and, if the programming is good, it produces the action we desire. Sloppy programming, whether on a computer or in a conversation, can confuse the situation, produce the wrong outcome, and even mess things up somewhere else.

The good news is that, just as you can put a new program on your laptop or mobile device, you can reprogram your conversation code.

The first step is to be conscious of conversations – especially the ones *you* are part of.

Do Try This At Home

Consider the activities of your day-to-day work, and identify the people you collaborate with, whose work influences yours, or whose work you may influence.

Select one of them as the subject of your fieldwork. This person will be a contributor to your success. Over the next few days, track and examine all your communication with them. Your aim is to get a sense of the frequency, nature, and quality of your communication with this one individual. The following questions can be your guidelines.

1. How many times a week did you talk using the following means?

   - Telephone
   - email
   - Face-to-face, just the two of you
   - Face-to-face, in group meeting

2. How many times did you start the communication?

3. How many times did your selected contact start the communication?

4. How many interactions were required to get the work done, the mystery solved, or the matter settled?

5. Does the very act of being aware of your communication with this person change it, in some way? How?

A Powerful Business Tool

As he walked down the hall that led to Emma Bateman's office, Paul was apprehensive. Though they had both served on an industry committee when Emma was in her previous job, he didn't really know much about the new CEO. He knew she didn't waste time, got difficult things done, and was very, very smart. Seven months earlier, Forthright Financial had hired her after the previous CEO retired prematurely and suddenly. She'd arrived with an impressive résumé and a good reputation in the industry. Investment analysts shared the view of the board of directors that the company had been lucky to recruit her into the top job. She soon earned a reputation, inside Forthright, as smart, fair, and a bit quirky.

When he learned what was on her mind, Paul figured it was the quirky element at work.

"What I'm about to propose might strike you as slightly weird," she said, "but hear me out. I think you'll see the logic. Pretty much the only reason I was brought in to do this job is that nobody in the organization was ready to take over when Gord Flannery retired. His early departure was a wake-up call for the board because it showed them they hadn't paid enough attention to leadership development and succession planning. Part of my job is to make sure that doesn't happen again. We need a strong leadership team that's ready for anything. For the board and for me, developing leaders is a top priority. We have to develop them everywhere in this company."

Paul was pretty sure where the conversation was going next. He'd been a solid performer for 10 years at Forthright and was ready for more challenge. A promotion to the executive ranks made perfect sense. He would welcome a larger salary, stock options, a dedicated parking spot, and the usual executive goodies. Jenny would be pleased too – less worry about funding the girls' education. Better yet, he'd see the last of Project Delta. Nothing weird about that.

Emma continued. "Right now, I have a bigger headache. Project Delta. To put it nicely, it's a mess."

Paul winced. Fantasy over.

Emma glanced at a pile of papers on her desk. "I see re-plan after re-plan. I listen to excuses and accusations. I read the weekly reports that take all week to decipher. You'd think we were trying to put a man on the moon. It's a sales system, not rocket science. Does anyone have a clue what's going on? I sure don't."

Paul searched for a response. Emma saved him the trouble.

"If the story I'm getting is this bad, I figure it's got to be really ugly when it's not all prettied up for the boss. I've been doing some investigating. I have my ways to beat the CEO suck-up problem. The impression I get is that the technological challenges pale in comparison to the leadership and communication problems. Is that fair to say?"

"I'm not that familiar with the coding challenges. Integration shouldn't be a problem, once we get there," he said. The conversation was not going the way Paul had hoped. "You might want to talk to Taylor. And Burt, for sure."

Emma stood. "Here's the deal. I've seen you at work. You like solving problems. You are the only person on the team with the experience and smarts to get this sorted out. And, frankly, you're the only person nobody's mad at."

"I'd love to see your research," Paul said, trying to sound light-hearted.

Emma didn't smile. "Here's what I need from you. I need your help to get this project moving again. Don't worry. I'm not expecting you to do Burt's job. He's got unique technical skills and we're too far down the path to be messing with that. I need you to help him. I need you to share the project manager role to facilitate collaboration and communication. Both seem to be missing on this project. I know he's prickly, but not all the trouble is Burt's fault."

Paul felt ill. The idea of sharing a role with Burt Shepler was painful. It absolutely would not work. He'd quit before he'd work with that oaf. His head hurt. He watched Emma's lips moving without hearing a thing she said.

She was explaining that this was a good opportunity. Build a communication culture within a team that could be extended through the organization. "Scalable! Isn't that the word you IT guys use? We can roll it out, just like software."

Is she crazy? Paul wondered. Or does she think I am?

Emma continued in the mode of visionary CEO rallying the troops. "If there's one thing I've learned in 30 years in this business, it's that leadership needs communication. It's good for a leader to be smart. Maturity helps. Education and experience are great, along with self-awareness, confidence, emotional intelligence, and all that good stuff. But, more than anything, a leader has to be able to communicate."

The knot in Paul's stomach tightened. Communication was not one of his strengths. It was an ever-present area for improvement on his performance reviews dating back as long as he could recall. Once he'd responded by contacting the training department, who put him on a presentation skills course. It was moderately interesting and improved his slide shows. Apart from that, he rarely gave communication much thought. Wasn't it something people just do instinctively? You're either a born communicator or you're not. He was not.

"When I talk about communication," Emma said, "I'm talking about really making contact with people. You understand them. They understand you. You both understand the situation and what needs to happen. In this organization, people seem to think communication begins with memos and ends with slide presentations. In between, there are meetings so formatted and full of reports, there's no room for discussion. And we all get five million emails a day, give or take a few. The sort of communication that's missing around here is real conversation."

Emma paused, walked to the white board and neatly printed: Conversation = business tool. She turned her attention to Paul. "That's where you fit in."

Paul looked at the board, then at Emma. "I'm not sure I get it," he said, ashamed to admit his confusion, especially to the CEO.

"Exactly!" she said. "That's why you're perfect for this project. Trust me. It will make sense in time. It will transform your career and maybe your life. Frankly, I'm hoping it'll do the same for me."

Paul was slightly curious. Perhaps he was regaining consciousness. "OK, Emma. You have my attention."

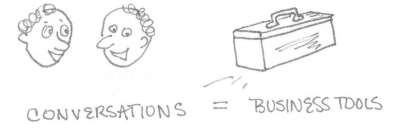

She continued. "Question: What is the main purpose of your job?"

"Technology integration." Surely Emma knew that.

"And just what does that mean, in English?"

"I and my team make sure that the tools everyone relies on to do their jobs actually work the way they're supposed to. We keep an eye on technology developments, inside and outside the company. And we bring in or upgrade the tools that will help people do their jobs better."

Emma was smiling. "So your job is to find and implement new business tools."

"Yeah, you could say that. They have to show value, meet cost/benefit hurdles, and such. There's a lot of up-front analysis."

Emma's smile broadened. "They're necessary. And they're useful. And they're cost-effective. And they're business tools." She pointed to the white board.

Paul read it out loud. "Conversation equals business tool." He paused. "Oh no, Emma, we do technology. We don't do people stuff."

"Everyone does people stuff," Emma said, "unless we're not human. The last time I checked, we weren't using robots. Are we? I guess you'd know better than I would."

Paul had to laugh. "No robots, yet. They're certainly available if you're interested."

"I'll stick with what we've got. Right now that's people." Emma reached for a black binder, overflowing on every side, and passed it to Paul. "Here's some research I pulled together when I joined Forthright. There are comments from employee opinion surveys, summaries of interviews with employees who leave, focus group data, and some relevant articles."

A yellowed photocopy drifted out of the binder and landed on the floor. The headline read, "Communication Is My Job." Paul noticed the article was from 1993.

"There's nothing there that will surprise you except that we've known this for so long and haven't done anything about it," Emma said. "People want to know what they're supposed to be doing and how well they're doing it. They want to know where their work fits into the bigger picture and what that picture looks like. They want to know how they're doing. They want to know that someone notices. They want to know what happens if they need help."

At that moment, Paul thought he could use some help. He didn't have a clue where the conversation was going and not knowing always made him uncomfortable. He still had no idea what, apart from nobody being mad at him, had caused Emma to pick him for the job.

Emma continued. "They don't get that sort of info from newsletters and videos and memos. Not even from the ones that win awards, like ours do. One article in the file suggests that formal communications, like *Forthright Focus*, have the least impact, though they get most of an organization's attention. Instead, employees get most of the information they need from their managers. More precisely, they get it from what their managers say and do – or don't say and don't do. And sometimes they don't get the message at all. Or they misunderstand it. Or they get the wrong one."

Paul winced as he thought of his own team and how often they seemed confused. He wondered what role he was playing in that.

"Our own survey data lines up pretty closely with data from other organizations," Emma said. "But that's not where we want to be. The middle of the pack isn't where we *"mavericks"* hang out." She used her fingers to put "mavericks" in quotation marks, as if she didn't believe the corporate myth. "There are lots of reasons to change, not the least of which is the impact of good communication on the bottom line – better profits, higher productivity, lower turnover, higher morale, better service, et cetera."

Paul flipped through the binder. Emma had certainly done her homework. There was a lot of information there, with highlights and many margin notes in Emma's handwriting. It was clear that this was important to her. But tying it to Project Delta? Insanity!

"Paul, people in this company need better communication. Managers, employees, branches, head office, even technology integration directors and CEOs. We need to understand each other if we're going to do our jobs better. We especially need to communicate if we're going to be leaders and develop new leaders. We can't do it with emails and slideshows."

Paul remembered the last Project Delta meeting. Burt's presentation had had 58 slides. He'd counted.

"There's a lot of communication activity going on here," she said, pointing to the pile of memos and reports on her desk, "but there's precious little real communication. The system needs an upgrade."

Paul was getting more and more uncomfortable. "I won't argue against the need, but isn't that a job for Human Resources or the folks in Corporate Communications?"

"I won't say they couldn't do it, and we'll certainly involve them, but both departments have an image problem. Even though it's not true, these guys are seen as being out of the loop. Everything they do looks like a

"Program" with a capital P." Emma quoted with her fingers again. "People think they're management fads, not critical to our operations. If we're going to change the way people communicate in this company, it's never going to happen through a capital-P program. It has to come from the heart of the organization in the day-to-day work. It's got to be systemic, incremental, like a series of computer system upgrades. You and your group organize those every day. That's another reason I thought of you."

Now she was dragging his team into this communication business. Paul tried to think of a tactful way to explain to Emma that he and they would make a bigger hash of her project than HR and PR could do in her worst nightmares. He didn't know the first thing about human communication. The team seemed to know even less. Data communication through phones and networks? Yes. People? Forget it.

"Paul, I know you don't consider yourself a brilliant communicator. That's what makes you perfect for this job. You're like everyone else. You can relate to the problem. You have the problem. We need to create something that works for people like you and me. We're busy people involved in a million projects who interact with all sorts of people. We need to help those people understand what's going on so we can all make this organization work."

Emma had already organized resources. Paul could add another employee, on contract, to add to his team's capacity. Gita Vish, the HR director, and Joe Granberg, head of Corporate Communications, would advise as needed. There was a budget for research and outside training and a generous amount for contingency. Emma seemed to have pre-empted all Paul's logical objections. His inner voice was screaming, "But this is not what I do!"

"This is where you're going to think I'm totally off my rocker," Emma said, after an uncharacteristically long pause. "I've arranged one more resource for you. There's a café on Wellington Street where you can get a lot of help with this project."

Given the nature of the assignment and his obvious lack of qualifications, Paul found the prospect of finding help in a coffee shop no nuttier than what Emma had already proposed. In the unlikely event he took on this task, he was going to need all the help he could get. If he could pick up help along with a cup of decaf, so much the better. He couldn't rely on his usual pattern of going it alone, drawing up a good plan, and making things happen through hard work and willpower.

"The café owner, Katy De Marco, is no ordinary barista," Emma continued. "She was our corporate counsel where I used to work, one of the sharpest minds on our team. She got bored or fed up or restless or had a midlife crisis or something and took early retirement the minute she was eligible. She travelled for a while – exotic places, Latin America, Africa, Asia. Then, one day, she calls me up and invites me over for a coffee. I head downtown to what I expect will be a law office and instead, it's this amazing café and Katy owns it."

Emma held up a mug. Printed on the side were the words: Drink + Think = The Coffee Grounds.

"But the coffee's only a sideline. She's consulting. Or coaching. I'm not sure what you'd call it. Anyways, she's good at it. She's helped me. Her vision is to create a better world by creating better workplaces. She figures we all spend so much time at work that it's the best place to start to make a difference in the world."

Paul calculated that, even working just 40 hours a week, it was about a third of a person's waking time. Katy's idea had merit. His mind wandered to his own situation. He wasn't sure he wanted to spend a third of his life working with Burt Shepler and turning people into communicators. Much too far outside his comfort zone. He'd update his résumé on the weekend. He still had good contacts. He could always go back to Denman's.

His stomach contracted at the thought of returning to his previous employer. OK, maybe not Denman's. The project management experience he'd gained at Forthright would be worth something. He was almost finished the MBA. That would look good to a recruiter. But the timing of this was just awful. He had a mortgage and a family. And he'd invested a lot of time and energy getting to where he was.

Emma was still singing Katy's praises. "She's got this knack for asking the question that, when you answer it, you have the answer to a bigger question. It's a question you hadn't thought of yet. Or you were afraid to ask it."

What Emma said next brought Paul's mind back into the conversation.

"I wouldn't be in this job, or any job, if it weren't for Katy. I was in a rut, back at the bank. I didn't notice because I was so busy being comfortable when I wasn't busy being overworked. She woke me up with one question. I didn't sleep for days. This was when she was still a lawyer, so it wasn't because of the caffeine."

Paul smiled. "What was the question?"

Emma looked right into his eyes, maybe deeper. "What one thing, if you could make it happen, would make you love your work?"

"So what was your answer?" This was starting to be interesting.

"I didn't know. I couldn't remember loving my work. I couldn't imagine loving my work. It really stumped me."

Paul guessed Emma wasn't used to being stumped. "Is that why you left?"

"No. It was years ago. I had excuses, namely a mortgage and a family, and a lot of time and energy invested in getting to where I was."

"I hear you," Paul said, wondering if the CEO had read his mind. "So how did Katy help you?"

"That's a story for another day. What's important, today, is that she can help you. If you agree. I know you're surprised and uncertain – maybe annoyed – about this assignment. I expected that. You're free to turn it down. I'll understand completely. But you might want to talk with Katy before you make your decision."

"You're right about the surprise. It's more like shock," Paul said. "I'll definitely need to give it a good, hard think. Can I let you know Monday?"

"Take as long as you need. Shall I tell Katy you'll be contacting her?"

Paul hoped Emma didn't notice how badly he wanted to get out of her office and get some air to clear his head. "Sure. Thanks. I'll let you know how it goes."

That evening, while heading home, he was still wondering about the question that had stumped Emma. What one thing, if you could make it happen, would make you love your work? He couldn't answer, either. He wondered if anyone at Forthright could.

What's Going On Here

The idea that conversation is a business tool may seem as surprising to you as it did to Paul. People generally think of tools in terms of tangible objects, such as a mobile phone, calculator, stethoscope or jackhammer. Each tool makes it possible or easier for the operator to do something connected with his or her work. It can be hearing a voice or a hearing a heartbeat, crunching numbers or crunching pavement.

Though we can't really see or touch them, computer applications are also office tools. These programs manipulate data and information to achieve an intended result, from a banking transaction to a slideshow. Some of them also connect people and ideas.

Think about a conversation. The process of discussion lets us manipulate data and information. It connects people and ideas. The processor just happens to be the human brain, not a computer chip. Most human beings have all the hardware and the software required for a face-to-face conversation: working brains, five senses, eyes, ears, and mouths.

If we were trying to create a user's manual for our inborn communication system (which is, in a way, what we are doing here) the first section would focus on knowing what you want to use it for. Just like a computer system, a well-executed conversation achieves an intended result.

Knowing what you want to happen is the foundation of requirements definition in building software. It's also the foundation and most critical aspect of a conversation. That's obvious, in theory. Unfortunately, in practice, unclear objectives are the biggest barriers to effective communication, formal or informal, spoken or written. If we're not crystal clear about what we want to achieve, we won't know what path to take to our goal, and we won't know when we've reached it.

Do Try This At Home

Once again, think of several people with whom you collaborate, whose work influences yours or whose work you may influence. Identify some of the things you communicate about. What's one of your desired outcomes from the communication?

Select one of these individuals as the subject of your fieldwork. This might be the person you chose for the exercise in Chapter 1.

1. Of the things you discuss with this person, which is the most important to your work or theirs?
2. What is one desired outcome for you with respect to this topic?
3. Why is it important? What does it mean for you and the organization?
4. What do you suppose is the other person's desired outcome?
5. What has to happen for your outcome to be achieved?
6. What has to happen for the other person's outcome to be achieved?
7. How will you know when you've reached that outcome?
8. How will the other person know?
9. What's your role in making all of this clear?
10. Besides getting the job done, what are other benefits of making it clear?

Ponder this: What one thing, if you could make it happen, would make you love your work?

CHAPTER

3

An Audience Of One

riday's Project Delta meeting was the usual ordeal. Even though Burt Shepler was out sick, he called in and using the speakerphone, added his views to everything said. Burt seemed to be trying to make up for his physical absence by talking more. He always had to have the last word, as if that was how he maintained his role as the leader, or reminded everyone of it. He gave two variations of his patented *"Well done! Heads will roll!"* speech. It would have been easy for Paul to accidentally on purpose disconnect him, but the meeting seemed to be ending on its own.

As he walked back to the main building, Lynnette Benson rushed to catch him. She'd been unusually quiet throughout the meeting. Paul was surprised he'd even noticed this, since he didn't usually keep track of people's participation. Nor did he generally pay much attention to Lynnette. She was just another of those noisy people from Marketing, squawking about customer satisfaction scores, and brandishing a calendar. They reminded him of Chicken Little, running around shouting: "The sky is falling!"

"Does it get better?" Lynnette asked.

"Does what get better? You mean the project?" Paul waited for the whining to begin. "At least the meeting ended on time today."

Lynnette wasn't whining. She looked exhausted. "I mean the longer you stay. Do you get used to it? You've been here, what, 10 years?"

"Close to it. You?" Paul realized he didn't know anything about Lynnette.

"Two years, to the day."

"Happy anniversary," Paul said, thinking that two years should be long enough to get used to anything. "Get used to what?"

"I don't know. Spinning your wheels. Wasting your time. Beating your head against a brick wall. Not really seeing anything for all your effort besides a paycheck. Not that I don't love to see that paycheck."

"You and me both." Paul hoped that might end the conversation. Did Lynnette know these were the very things that were troubling him? He could sense that she needed to talk. Perhaps he did, too. "What makes me think this isn't just about Project Delta?"

"You're right," she said. "It's bigger than the project, though it always seems more acute at these meetings. Project Delta has all the symptoms of something that seems like an epidemic around here. There are some brilliant minds around that table – nice people, hard workers, well intentioned, innovative, all that jazz. It's a worthwhile project with enough resources and it's almost certain to spin money for Forthright, once we get it done. It's just that, sometimes, it feels as if nobody has a clue what we're doing and nobody seems to care. Maybe I'm exaggerating, but we're all smart and lovely people and yet, somehow we're not living up to our potential."

"I get your point," Paul said, "though I don't think I've ever been called *lovely* before, and I'm sure the same is true for our fearless leader."

Lynnette didn't laugh. "I don't think Burt is the problem, though he sure contributes to it. I think it's all of us. We're all in our own little worlds, with our own little problems and agendas, and we're just not helping each other. Do you ever get that sense? Or am I nuts?"

"No, not nuts, unless we all are," said Paul. "You care. Sometimes it feels like you're the only one who does. Am I right? I'll admit I often feel that way, especially lately. Project Delta is like a lightning rod for everything that's wrong with Forthright. Your idea about us not living up to our potential and not helping each other is scary because there's truth in it. It's as if we're plugged in, but the connection isn't there."

"There's no energy," Lynnette said, her voice fading to a whisper.

"And no signal." As he said those words, Paul thought of the CEO, and the concerns she'd expressed the previous day. "We're not communicating. We're disconnected."

Paul found it bizarre that, for the second day in a row, he was engaged in a conversation about communication. He was, emphatically, not the person to consult on these things. His meeting with Emma had kindled some interest in his own interactions. Perhaps that was a step in the right direction. In his conversation with Lynnette, he'd opened up a little more than usual, admitted his own confusion, and confessed he didn't have the answers. That was not something he ever let his own group know, or his daughters. Managers and fathers had to know the answers. Or they had to act as if they did, even when they didn't.

He had to chuckle at how wrong that idea was, and wondered where it came from. It was an old one. He thought of his own father. He always knew the answers. Paul knew that, were his dad still alive, he'd say that was a load of nonsense. He didn't know all the answers. He was making it up as he went along, just as Paul was.

He'd booked the full afternoon for the Project Delta meeting and it had ended earlier than expected. He'd take a walk and grab a coffee before heading back to his office. It was a good excuse to check out The Coffee Grounds, as he'd promised Emma. It was an easy promise to keep. He loved coffee and a change of scenery would be good.

He walked the four blocks to the café, mindful of his other promise to Emma. To work more closely with Burt was bad enough. To seriously consider leading the charge in her dream to improve communication at Forthright? That one was hard to handle. As much as the idea was interesting and might be good for his career, he wasn't the right person for the job. How strange that Emma believed that his biggest liability, not being a good communicator, made him superbly qualified.

The aroma told him he'd arrived at The Coffee Grounds. It wasn't fancy, though it was impressive. Coffee was the main attraction here. At centre stage was a gleaming roaster, trimmed with copper and brass, the size of an old furnace. It was surrounded by burlap sacks filled, he assumed, with green coffee beans. Shelves of large glass jars held the roaster's dark, shiny output. The brewing area and cash register were to the left, behind a modestly stocked pastry counter complete with a display of large cookies and small chocolate bars. Sunbeams streamed into the main seating area, which awaited the after work crowd. The seating looked comfortable enough, but not like an invitation to lounge all afternoon. On the right was a smaller, more private area with just three tables.

A young woman stood behind the counter, tidying the cups. Not much over 20, she was too young to be Emma's friend, the lawyer/consultant/owner. "May I help you?" she said.

"Grande, half-caf, skinny with an extra shot," he said.

"Would you like a coffee with that?" The girl was smiling as she pointed to the last line on the chalkboard menu. It said: You don't need to learn a second language to get a coffee here!

"We don't speak barista babble," she said. "We're a jargon free zone."

"Well, that's good news. Let's make it a big decaf latte. Skim milk. No whipped cream or sprinkles or anything weird. To stay. How much?" Paul paid, waited for the coffee, then installed himself at a table by the window. The coffee was delicious, strong, not over-roasted, with a generous layer of dense foam. He pulled out the file Emma had given him and began skimming the articles. One suggested that employees learn more than 80 per cent of what they know about their jobs from everyday interactions with colleagues.[2] Another cited a survey that showed unclear objectives, lack of team communication, and ineffective meetings are among the top time wasters workers around the world say make them feel unproductive for as much as a third of their work week.[3]

Were things that bad at Forthright? He thought about the meeting he'd just left and knew it was possible. But how to fix it?

"Would you like a cookie?" A tall woman, older than the first, was crossing the room with a plate of biscotti. Judging by the delicious scent wafting towards him, they were not long out of the oven. "They're on the house at this particular moment. New recipe. I need some feedback."

"Thanks," Paul said. "But I have to warn you, I'm hard to please."

"Then you're perfect for the job."

Paul welcomed the interruption and helped himself to one of the cookies, fragrant and loaded with almonds. He swirled it through his coffee and took a foamy bite. "Keep that recipe," he said. "These are great."

"Can I bring you another latte?"

"No thanks. To be honest, I'm not really here for the coffee, though it's super. Emma Bateman sent me. I'm Paul Hunchak."

"I was hoping you were. As you probably suspected, I'm Katy De Marco." She offered her hand. Katy's firm, confident handshake was no surprise. Everything about her supported Emma's description of an unusual ally. "Nice to meet you. Will you join me?"

Katy took the spare wicker chair at his table. "Emma told me a bit about your communication project. It sounds like fun."

"Fun? Maybe in Emma's mind but it's still her project, not mine," said Paul. "If you ask me, and I know you didn't, I'm the last man on earth who should be teaching people to be communicators."

"What makes you say that?"

"Because I'm a lousy communicator. I don't mind writing, but I'm just no good at all that touchy-feely stuff. I'm a systems guy. And an accountant. I'm not a people person. I can communicate when I think about it. But I don't think about it very often, quite frankly."

"You and millions of others. So, why do you think Emma picked you?"

"Desperation? Insanity? Cruelty? Punishment for some unknown sin?"

"I'm serious," said Katy. "If you were trying to create a program to help people who aren't gifted communicators figure it out, who would you put in charge?"

"The Training Department. Not me." Paul wasn't budging. He was wrong for this job and that was the end of it.

Katy didn't seem to buy his argument. "What happens if Emma puts the trainers on the case?"

"It would be a two-day offsite with a bunch of exercises. There'll be a video with starfish or Swiss watches or that fellow from *Monty Python*. We'll do some annoying role-plays. We'll get a 400-slide presentation and a nice looking binder. Group hug at the end. Then we'll all go back to the job, get swamped by work, and forget it all." Paul had minimal experience with the training department, but he was sure a communication training program would be soft, fluffy, and useless.

"What? No rope climbing or colorful costumes?" Katy laughed. "I can see you don't think much of their chances of getting it right. Neither did Emma. Seriously, why do you guess she picked you?"

"No guessing, really. She told me." Paul had forgotten Emma's actual words and remembered only his own interpretation. "I'm a lousy communicator. She has this nutty idea that this is a job for someone just like the people it aims to help. It's the blind leading the blind or, in this case, the dumb leading the dumb. She dug up a stressed-out middle manager who doesn't have a clue."

Katy looked serious. "If you'll let me share an observation, I'd say you do have a clue. Most managers have lots of clues. They ignore them because they think they're too busy. Communication is an essential human skill. It's in our DNA. Last week, I read about a study that showed we're hard-wired to communicate. We're designed to be social. Unfortunately, nobody ever teaches us how to do communication well. We learn by osmosis and if we aren't exposed to good interpersonal communication in action, we never really learn it."

"Some people are good at it," Paul said, thinking of Jenny. "My wife is a born communicator. I almost always know what's going on with her and what she wants."

Katy nodded. "I'm guessing she learned from life experience. You can bet she didn't learn it in school. We don't get formal instruction in how to talk with each other. Did you? I sure didn't. They teach us all sorts of stuff about how the language works: how to conjugate verbs, change tenses, and make the noun agree with the verb. They teach us not to end a sentence with a preposition – which is utter crap – and where to put the commas. They even teach us to speak other languages. But have you ever heard of a school that teaches you how to conduct a meaningful conversation in any language?"

Paul had to admit he hadn't.

"It's no wonder more than half the population of just about any company, from the CEO to the gardener, says communication needs to improve. We shouldn't be surprised that so many managers are not good communicators. They never really learned how to do it." Katy's passion for the topic was evident. "Maybe they learned from really bad examples. Or they think it's hard, or they don't have time, or they just can do soft stuff."

"That's precisely what's worrying me about this project," said Paul. "I'm no good at that soft stuff."

"And you have proof of that?" Katy asked

"Well, not exactly."

"Then how do you know?"

"Communicating has always shown up on my performance reviews as an area for improvement. But I don't have real evidence, if that's what you're asking."

Katy smiled. "And without substantial evidence, you've concluded that you're bad at communication and can't learn?"

"OK, you caught me. I may have made an assumption." Paul wasn't sure he liked where this conversation was going.

"And might something else be true?"

"It's possible. But I don't have any evidence for that either."

"So, let's see if I get this," Katy said. "You don't need any evidence to believe you're a bad communicator, yet you need evidence to believe it might be otherwise?"

Paul knew he'd lost this round. "I see what you mean. It's not very logical, is it?"

"So what else might be true?"

"OK, maybe I could learn."

"How do you know?"

"Hey, I thought you were on my side. First, you seem to think we can learn it. Plus I've learned other things that I thought I never could."

"Such as?"

Paul paused. "Play the guitar."

"And how did you learn?"

"I wanted to play and sing for my daughters, so I was motivated. I had a book that showed me the basics and a teacher who encouraged me. I just kept messing around, making mistakes, and practicing till I got it. I guess it was trial and error, or experimenting. It helped that babies are a very forgiving audience."

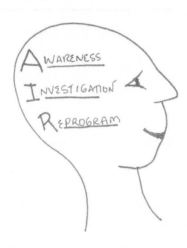

Katy took a paper napkin and drew a circle. Then she wrote the letters A, I and R on the right. "This is your brain," she said, pointing to the circle.

"Great, I'm an airhead," said Paul.

"Show me the evidence," Katy said. "Remember, I'm a recovering lawyer. Inside our heads, all the time - I mean 24 hours a day, even in our sleep – there's a conversation going on. We're talking to ourselves. This is the most important conversation we ever have, since it shapes every conversation we have with other people. Unfortunately, in that internal dialogue we're sometimes spouting nonsense. It's worth checking now and then."

"I'm not a psychologist, but I've been reading a lot about how the brain works. Our brains are programmed to look for patterns so they can make sense out of what's happening. When we have experiences or thoughts, our brains search their data banks for similar patterns. Thinking the same thought, over and over, sets up a neural pathway connecting a point in the brain with another point, one idea with another. The more you think it, the stronger the connection. It becomes the only thought you have on the matter. It's like walking the same path so often that you wear a groove so deep you can't get out."

"I'm pretty sure I've been in that position," said Paul.

"That's good, because the first step is to be aware of your self-talk." Beside the A on her drawing, Katy wrote: AWARE.

"Step two is to check that self-talk to determine if it's true. Inquire, investigate, interrogate. Pick one of them. That's what the I is for."

"Investigate works for me," Paul said, "I always head for the middle ground."

Katy wrote the word. "What do you think the R is for?"

"Run away?"

"Nice try, smart guy. Let's try reprogram. I think you know a thing or two about reprogramming."

Paul took the napkin. "So we notice that we're running an idea in our head, like a computer script. That's the awareness part. We investigate the script for accuracy and see how it's working for us. That's the "I" part. We write a new script. That's the reprogramming. Then, with any luck, we run the new script and get a better result."

"I'm all out of gold stars," said Katy. "Would you like another cookie?"

"No thanks. Spoils my dinner. Doesn't this AIR thing oversimplify the situation?"

"Absolutely! It's a model, not science. My point is that you only think you're a lousy communicator because you've been thinking that thought for ages. You're clearly capable of learning. The guitar's just one example. The art of a real conversation is something you can learn. Anyone can. And when you take on Emma's challenge …"

Paul held up his hand. "Whoa! If, not when, I take it."

"… you'll not only be giving Forthright and everyone in it, including yourself, a brilliant business tool, you'll probably be the only person in the world who's getting paid to learn how to talk to people. How cool is that?"

"Not cool enough to make me want to risk my career by working closely with Burt Shepler. And this communication stuff is so far out of my domain. What if I blow it?"

"You won't blow it. Emma won't let you. I won't let you. You won't let you. You're the guy who makes complicated systems work. Think of workplace conversation as just another complicated system."

"First Emma, now you, spouting this *communication is a system* idea. Even my wife, Jenny, used it last night, when I told her about Emma's idea. Are you all in the same cult or something? I don't see it. A system is predictable. There's a process. Communication is random, not something you can control."

"And you think that because …?"

"People are unpredictable."

"Always?"

"Pretty much?"

"Are you unpredictable?"

Paul thought for a moment. "No. I'm actually pretty consistent."

"I see." Katy smiled and took a cookie. "Are you a freakish exception to the rule?"

Paul couldn't decide if Katy was absolutely brilliant or simply annoying. "OK, I see where you're going. I'm assuming people are unpredictable, but when you look at it, we all have our operating patterns. I still don't see how that makes communication like a system."

"Well," said Katy, "it's not quite as reliable as the sort of systems you work with, but there are ways to structure conversations so they do the job you need them to do, whether it's to exchange information, make a decision, build trust, or whatever. There are techniques you can learn. Anyone can."

"You have evidence?" Paul said.

"I've seen it happen many times. I've also seen what happens when people don't have a process and don't see the patterns. Confusion, bad decisions, mistrust, wrecked relationships. Bad stuff all around."

"Yeah, we've all seen that. And it's rampant, if you believe this stuff in Emma's file."

Katy looked at Paul searchingly: "Do you believe it?"

"Some of it's probably junk science. But some of the research looks reliable. It's stuff I always knew in my gut, but now that I've seen real data on it, well, I guess it's more serious than I thought."

"So what's behind your resistance to getting involved? You could make a real difference."

"You really *are* in cahoots with my wife. She said the same thing, last night."

"You didn't answer my question. Where's the resistance coming from? It's not really about qualifications or experience, is it?"

"Technically, I'm probably no less qualified than anyone else on the team." Paul tried to find the words to explain his nagging fear. He was surprised he'd admit it to a stranger. "What makes me queasy is that it all feels so personal."

"How so?"

"I get through life by being competent. I'm good with ideas and research and coming up with solutions to problems. But they're business problems and technical problems, not people stuff."

Katy nodded. "I think that when you dig into Emma's file you'll find that there's a relationship between the people stuff and business problems. Is it possible that your concern is that Emma's asked you to step outside your zone of competence, your comfort zone?"

"Could be, but it'd be right into the Discomfort Zone," said Paul. "To boldly go where no man has gone before."

Katy laughed. "Except that this isn't Star Trek and I'm pretty sure you've been to the Discomfort Zone a time or two. You beamed back safely. You've seen what happens when competence teams up with courage. It's pretty powerful."

The mention of courage made Paul uncomfortable. He checked his watch. "I'd better get back to the office. I still have a job to do, and Emma's big fat research file to read."

"And then?" said Katy.

"I told Emma I'd let her know on Monday. It's going to be an interesting weekend as I read the file and mull it all over and…"

"And interrogate your self-talk?" Katy asked.

"Sure thing. Thanks for that idea; for the whole conversation. Things don't look quite as bleak as they did when I came in."

"My pleasure. Let me know what you decide. See you Monday?"

"Save me a cookie," said Paul.

What's Going On Here

Katy's assertion that the conversation you have with yourself is the most important addresses the third step in becoming an effective communicator. Once you're aware of your communication (Chapter One) and know what you're trying to achieve in a conversation (Chapter Two) you need to be clear of old biases, false assumptions and old scripts as Paul calls them, that don't serve your purpose any more.

Negative self-talk is one of the highest barriers to great performance. If we don't feel it's possible to do great work, we can't do it. Nor can we do it if we think we're engaged in a solitary struggle and nobody appreciates our efforts. When we examine and challenge these beliefs about ourselves and others, we can remove inaccurate information and provide an uncluttered space for holding conversations with others. We have to do it often, since the old scripts, memorized long ago, resurface until they're replaced with new ones.

Lynnette's observation that the people at Forthright aren't living up to their potential reflects the situation in organizations everywhere. If we don't believe the people around us care about their work, about our own work or about us, it's almost impossible to be motivated. If we're telling ourselves that others don't care and aren't supporting us, we can feel like victims. Our stories of victimhood prevent us from operating at a level anywhere near our potential. If Lynnette is starting to feel like a victim, you can bet others are, too.

It's helpful to examine the evidence and challenge our assumptions.

Our investigations may show us that something else could be true. That particular something can be a great starting place for improving the situation. Recognizing that other possibilities exist helps us reprogram our thoughts. Then we can see meaning in our work and a purpose to what we are doing.

Organizations have a role to play in this reprogramming. It's not enough to say, "Employees are our greatest asset," and "We care about our customers," and "Quality is our highest priority." They have to mean it, they have to do it, and they have to show it. As employees, when we go looking for evidence that our work is more than just a paycheck, we'll only find it if our employers operate in ways that demonstrate those statements are true.

Do Try This At Home

The first task is to examine your self-talk. Think about a work situation you're involved in that's causing you some concern or isn't unfolding the way you'd like. Practice the AIR technique.

What is the situation?

- A = Awareness – What are you telling yourself about the situation? How are you describing your role in it? Are these explanations supporting you and meeting your objectives?
- I = Inquire, Investigate, Interrogate – Is what you are telling yourself true? What evidence do you have? Could something else be true? What else might that be?
- R = Reprogram – Think about alternate explanations that better serve you and your objectives. Write these helpful explanations down and read them out loud. This helps you to create new links in your brain.

The next time you notice you're telling yourself the same old story, you'll think of these new stories.

Note: Reprogramming isn't the same as parroting positive affirmations, such as, "I'm beautiful and successful," with the hope they'll come true.

Instead, you're introducing your brain to new possibilities, upgrading your thinking process to use all the information available, not just what's in the old familiar stories.

The second part of your fieldwork is to examine how you learn. Not everyone learns in the same way. What methods work for you?

Think of something you learned to do as an adult. What motivated you to learn it? How did you learn to do it? What was the process you used?

Which of these processes works best for you: reading, watching someone, talking about it, trial and error?

Knowing your style helps you figure out how to approach your own learning. If you have a drawer full of unread software and appliance manuals, you probably don't learn through reading and may not benefit from how-to or self-help books. On the other hand, you may be very successful with a live teacher, coach or mentor, who can explain, discuss or model the behaviour you want to learn. If you learn best by trying something for yourself, nothing will substitute for experience.

Some activities lend themselves to a certain way of learning. We don't want to ride on a bus where the driver learned all he knows about the job from reading the Highway Code or the vehicle's owner's manual.

When it comes to communication, reading, watching and discussing the principles also have value, yet real world practice is the best way to become proficient.

———•◦•———

CHAPTER

4

The Things You Can Control

"I want you to promise to ask for help when you need it," Emma had told Paul Monday morning when he called to say he'd take on her project. "I suspect that won't be easy for you."

"Why do you say that?"

"Because you're a Lone Ranger. I used to be one. But you can't do a job like mine or yours on your own. I'll bet you see yourself as a capable, independent individual who makes things happen – alone. You don't want anyone, including you, to think you don't have all the answers. Feels like incompetence." She paused, looked at Paul to see if she had struck a nerve, and continued.

"But it's not about competence. Nobody has all the answers, especially in something like this project. Asking for help when you need it is a whole lot smarter than struggling alone. My life improved at least 100 per cent when I started sharing the load. Remember, even the Lone Ranger had a sidekick."

Later that day, back in his office, Paul thought about what Emma had said. He had a hard time picturing her as the loyal Tonto riding beside him across the plain, righting wrongs and fighting bad guys. Yet she had read him correctly. He'd spend hours puzzling over a problem rather than call someone who might know the answer. Would he feel comfortable calling on the CEO? Not likely. But this job didn't seem to be about comfort. Perhaps this was something he could get over, as Emma claimed to have done.

Will I really look incompetent if I ask for help? That sounded like a question to include in that self-talk exercise Katy had shown him. He wasn't convinced this coaching business was going to work. Still, Emma was tossing good money at the idea, so he'd give it a chance. He had to admit Katy was interesting. Would she be useful?

He'd tried her self-talk exercise on the weekend as he debated whether to take the assignment. What were the words she had drawn beside AIR on that napkin? Awareness. Investigation. Reprogramming. Examining and challenging his beliefs was unfamiliar and uncomfortable. Yet he had to admit there wasn't much evidence to support some of them. What was true? Project Delta was a mess but not past salvaging. Burt Shepler was arrogant and thoughtless but not the monster Paul imagined him to be. He'd worked with other difficult characters. Surely he could work with Burt. It wasn't forever.

At that moment, the phone rang. It was Burt. By now, he would have heard from Emma that Paul would be playing a bigger role on Project Delta.

"Apparently Emma thinks I need your help. Do you know what that's about? With all respect, personally, I think what we need is more time. And more people who know what they're doing."

Paul wondered if that last question was intended to insult him.

"I won't argue about the time," he said. "But I do think our people do know what they're doing. Emma wants us to get them doing it better. My role is to explore communication, teamwork, how we work together."

"Well, as long as you stick to the touchy-feely stuff," Burt said. "I'm still in charge of this project."

"I'm pretty sure we can figure it out." Paul wasn't sure they could, but he sensed this was not the time to argue about control. "Let's book some time to talk about how we'll make it work. The booking system shows we both have time available Thursday mornings. Perhaps we could schedule an hour, next week, and shorter weekly meetings, after that."

Silence. Paul could almost see Burt rolling his eyes. "I guess I can make it work, if that's what Emma wants . . . ."

"Great. I'll book Conference B for 9:00 every Thursday. See you there."

He'd bought some time. By Thursday he'd figure out how to handle the conversation. He wasn't thrilled to be working with Burt, and Burt would be even less enthusiastic. Since Emma's fingerprints were all over this assignment, Burt might see Paul as a threat to his status. It would be a difficult conversation.

He pulled out an article from Emma's file. There it was, *SCARF: A brain-based model for collaborating with and influencing others.*[4] The author cited discoveries in neuroscience suggesting the key to collaboration lay in using the brain's natural tendency to minimize threat and maximize reward. The human experiences of status, certainty, autonomy, relatedness and fairness neatly formed the acronym SCARF. Get SCARF right and you could reduce people's stress and gain their attention, support and collaboration.

"Status is about relative importance to others," he read. "Certainty is the ability to predict the future. Autonomy provides a sense of control over events. Relatedness is a sense of safety with others, rather friend than foe. And fairness is a perception of fair exchanges between people."

He was surprised to read that, for the brain, a threat to status is as serious as a physical threat. Would Burt's stress levels rise if he saw Paul as having more status because the CEO had put him on the project? What Burt thought was Burt's problem. Or was it?

As for certainty, there wasn't much of that on Project Delta, but some things could be predicted. How he and Burt would work together was one of them. Realistic expectations and a schedule might help.

Autonomy? Hmm. Having to share the project management role would reduce Burt's control. Would getting clear about who would do what ease that? They'd need that anyway.

Relatedness: there was a challenge. He didn't know anything about the guy except that he was hard to get along with. Would it be enough to have a shared sense of purpose? Could they even share that?

And what about fairness? How could this possibly look fair? Paul was coming in to what had been Burt's project. The only thing to do was to make sure he gave Burt something in exchange. But what? A successful project would do it. Less friction on the way there? Maybe a lesson or two in how to get along with people? Was that even possible?

The idea of a project to improve communication was starting to intrigue Paul. The articles in Emma's file told him the need was real. On the weekend, he'd spent time on the Internet, hunting for credible success stories of similar projects. No luck. People were talking about the need to improve face-to-face communication at work. If it was actually happening, he couldn't find much about it, though there was ample evidence that Forthright had lots of company in dysfunctional communication.

He'd found references to research showing employees don't leave companies, they leave bad bosses.[5] Others suggested most bad bosses are poor communicators.[6] He found a few references to studies that showed immediate supervisors are employees' preferred source of information about their organizations.[7] Other writers warned that it was dangerous to assume that bosses are the best source for all information. Yikes! If the experts couldn't agree on something as fundamental as who employees want to hear from, how was he, a total know-nothing where communication was concerned, going to make an impact on communication at Forthright?

He had been surprised that the word *conversation* derived from *turn about together*. He painted a mental image of people turning to face each other. Face-to-face and side-by-side, that's how collaboration takes place.

Another surprise was that the original meaning of *communicate* was to make common, as in something people can share. Another old meaning was *to connect,* as in, "the rooms communicated through a common hallway." Old fashioned language, but the notion of connection might be useful.

It was no surprise that he'd never given a thought to the meaning of these words. What was surprising was how little serious thought he had given to communication at all. He thought about communication when he had to write a proposal or a letter or if he was making a presentation. What would happen if he gave every conversation that sort of attention? It would definitely slow him down. Was that a bad thing?

He recalled the discussion he'd had that morning with his own group, after telling Emma he'd accept her challenge. It hadn't gone well. He'd called a hurried meeting, explained Emma's request and shared some of the facts and figures that showed the need and the benefits. He'd been careful to explain that a contract employee would be added to ease the workload impact and would start in a few weeks.

But workload wasn't their concern. Tom Demitrios had angrily summed it up by saying he hadn't become a systems engineer so he could do "fluffy stuff." Without time to sort out what seemed to be an emotional issue, Paul had replied, without thinking, "Fluffy or not, it's what Emma Bateman wants and it's what we're doing."

In hindsight, Paul knew that hadn't been the right thing to say. Had he known when he said it? Now that he thought about it, what he said, and how he said it violated most of the SCARF principles. It abdicated responsibility and avoided discussion. And if he was being honest, nor was it the right way to introduce the project to the very people whose support he needed to make it work. Making the project look like a CEO edict, when it wasn't – what kind of move was that? Now, he'd have to do a patch up job. He hated that. Was it always this much harder to recover from a communication blunder than to prevent it?

He had scheduled a 4:30 meeting with Katy at The Coffee Grounds, and was looking forward to it. She, at least, was on his side. They'd agreed she would be his coach as long as the project lasted, serving as a sounding board, providing an observer's perspective and administering, in her words, "butt kicking as required." Paul thought he needed a bit of a kick now, given the way he'd introduced his team to the project.

He arrived at the café just as Katy was emerging from the kitchen with a plate of cookies. "New concoction," she said, "Chocolate Chaos."

"Chaos is my theme today," Paul said. "I'll have one – and a latte."

"Skim milk, right?" Katy launched the steamer while Paul moved to a table for two in the small, quiet area of the café.

A minute later, Katy arrived with two steaming cups, and joined him. "What's up? What's causing your chaos?"

"Well, since I called Emma and told her I'm on board, I've started looking for a life jacket. Not sure this boat will float."

"Is that true?"

"Well. the project's intriguing. I read Emma's file and have to admit improving communication at Forthright – if we can get it right – will have a huge payoff. That's the good news. What I didn't find in the file, on the Internet, or in my brain was a clear path to get there. I didn't expect to Google *communication at work* and come up with a magic formula. But I did think there might be more examples of people doing it well. I'm not sure where to start."

He looked at Katy, who said nothing.

"So I was already a bit confused, and then I met with my own team. They are not buying into this project at all."

"What were you expecting?" Katy asked.

"I expected a little resistance, but they're downright ornery. It's as if they think this project is somehow beneath them. Some of them were kind of emotional about it. To be honest, it could be partly my fault. I didn't plan the conversation and I didn't leave enough time for questions. I thought the facts about the situation – and that it's Emma's idea – would be enough to convince them to get on board."

"Was that enough for you?"

"Hmm. I see your point. It took me a few days of thinking, a lot of reading, and a bunch of conversations with Emma, you, and my wife, before I was really on board."

"What do you think it's going to take for them?"

"It's definitely going to take another conversation, probably a few."

"Here's a question. What percentage of a conversation are you accountable for?"

"Fifty per cent?"

"Is that your final answer?"

Paul paused. "Is this a trick question?"

"What do you think?"

"Let's see. If you and I are in a conversation, each of us is responsible for half. One of us might do more of the talking, but the other one has a chance to be heard. I'll stick with 50 per cent."

"Would you believe this?" Katy asked, taking a paper napkin and writing on it: 100%!

"No, but I'll listen to your argument."

"In a conversation, whose activities can you control?"

Paul paused for a second. "Only mine. I can control what I say."

"Anything else?"

Paul drew a blank. "I guess I can control how I say it, my tone, and body language, if I think about it."

"Good. The way you sound and look are a huge part of your message. It almost doesn't matter what you say if you don't look like you mean it. There's a study somewhere that shows if how you look isn't consistent with what you say, people will believe what they see.[8] It's in our DNA or something. Is there anything else you can control?"

"Are we playing 20 Questions?" This was starting to be annoying, Paul thought. "What's your point?"

"My point," Katy said, "is that you can control a whole lot more than you think. What about when and where you have the conversation? What about the format – in a group or one-to-one? This is the environment of the conversation. You can control that."

"I'll give you that one. I guess if an important conversation starts and it's the wrong time or place or format, you can ask to move it. I never think of that. I usually just let it unfold, right there and then."

"Sometimes that works," Katy said. "It's good to know rescheduling is an option."

"Yeah. That would have helped this morning. I picked a bad time and when it didn't go the way I wanted it to, I just brought the discussion to a close."

"Does that pattern show up in other places in your life?"

Paul was silent. He thought of the Project Delta meetings, where his attempts to stop people from complaining often brought the meeting to an end. He wondered if he was like that at home with Jenny and the girls.

Katy continued. "Here's a big one. Can you control how you listen?"

"I guess you can." Paul was starting to get the picture. He thought back to the morning meeting and wondered if he or anyone had really been listening. "But you can't control how other people listen to you."

"You don't think so? I've seen managers create environments that help people listen, without defensiveness or emotion interfering with the signal."

"OK. How?"

"They started by letting go of their need to be right. It's a major barrier to real communication. If we think we have all the answers – or we're pretending to because we think that's part of our job – we aren't open to new ideas. We shut them down when they appear. If we recognize and admit that we're learning too, we make it safe for people to share their ideas and feelings. It builds trust and it encourages them to contribute their best. But we can't just say it; we have to mean it. Getting our egos out of the way takes some honest introspection. And some courage."

Paul knew Katy had struck a nerve. All his life, being right and having the answers were things he had expected of leaders: his father, his bosses, himself. He knew it was impossible, since they were all mortals, but it had become one of the Big Rules in his mind.

"Having to be right," Paul said. "That's an old story I've been telling myself. Guess I need to reprogram that one."

"If you don't have to be right, what else could be true?"

"Please, don't say I have to be wrong. That will kill me. Maybe I have to be curious."

"And how does that feel?"

"A whole lot easier than having to be right all the time. I'm curious by nature. Thanks, Katy."

"You figured it out. I just ask questions. I'll warn you; giving up the need to be right isn't easy. I'm not there myself, but I'm playing with it."

"Let's go back to the 100 per cent issue," Paul said. "If I accept that I'm 100 per cent responsible for the conversation, is it really about being aware of how my communication affects other people?"

"Pretty close. Once you start taking better care of people in your conversations, they're more relaxed and open, and less likely to jump to conclusions or get defensive. You create an environment where people feel safe to be themselves."

"That issue of safety reminds me of one of Emma's articles," said Paul. "SCARF is a way to figure out what might be stressing people, so you can help them relax and focus on a real conversation."

"Oh, I'm glad you read that article. It's a powerful idea and useful. It's a good intro to how our brains work. Neuroscience is helping us understand all sorts of things about thinking and learning and communication."

"Did you give Emma that article?" Paul asked.

"Maybe. Where she got it isn't important. The important thing is that you read it and now you have another tool you can use on this project. When you take responsibility for communication, you can make a difference. Consciously or unconsciously, people learn from you. They become more accountable for their own communication. That's good for everyone, especially you, since your conversations become smoother, more focused and way more productive. But until they see someone modeling the behavior, it's hard for people to imagine what it might look like."

"I'm not sure I'm the right role model."

"You're their best hope, right now."

"So, as a manager or a leader, I've got to draw the picture."

"Or be the picture." Katy spooned the last bits of foam from the bottom of her cup. "My first coach used to say, 'The meaning of your communication is the response you get.' Can you guess what he meant by that?"

Paul wasn't sure. "Would it mean that, no matter what I intend to say, people will provide their own meaning? I really don't know how they've interpreted my message until I see how they react?"

"Exactly. So what's your next step?"

"Head back to the office and look at the people, not just the facts. Instead of doing damage control on this morning's fiasco of a meeting, I'll see about creating that environment you talk about. This time, I'll be curious instead of right. And I'll focus on what they understand, not just what I say. Giving information isn't enough. I think I get that now."

"Good luck," Katy said. "Would you like some Chocolate Chaos for the road?"

What's Going On Here

As it was for Paul, the idea that one person is accountable for 100 per cent of a conversation can be hard for people to understand. Don't both parties have a share in sending and receiving messages? Of course, they do. But it isn't 50-50.

In an ideal world, both parties would feel accountable for 100 per cent of the interaction. You'd both make sure that the timing and place were right, that you built an environment of trust and confidence. You would address feelings as well as facts. Until that ideal world arrives, each of us can improve the conversations we're involved in by accepting that our words and actions influence how other people receive and understand us. The more consciously we prepare for our interactions, the more effectively we will communicate.

This sort of preparation can become a habit. Those who study such things claim that, with awareness and repetition, a new habit can be developed in a surprisingly short time. Like Paul, any one of us can learn a pattern of behavior that will create the conditions for understanding. Asking questions that reveal what people understand and what they plan to do is a good start.

- "What does that mean for you?"

- "How does that affect your work?"
- "What has to happen for that to work?"

Making a statement and asking, "Any questions?" seldom gives you a clue about whether and what people understood. Moreover, until you build a culture in which everyone knows questions are necessary and it is OK not to know the answer, some people may hold their questions, rather than admit they don't completely understand.

The phenomenon Katy calls "the need to be right" stops us from communicating effectively. If, in the past, we experienced negative consequences when we didn't know or were wrong about something – the sort of thing that happened to a lot of us in school – some part of our brain decided that we mustn't let it happen again. We must get things right. Afraid of being wrong, we become intolerant of views that don't support our own. Over time, dissenting voices around us stop, and we start believing we really are right. Unfortunately, dominating discussions and listening solely to our own voices, only increase our chances of being wrong.

Replacing the need to be right with the need to be curious opens our minds to possibilities. It invites others to participate with us in achieving goals. Removing the fear frees everyone to contribute from strengths, not conceal weaknesses.

The SCARF model, introduced by David Rock,[9] is a powerful tool to sensitize us to things that cause stress to us and to those we interact with. As leaders, everything we say, do, and decide has an impact on status, certainty, autonomy, relatedness, and fairness. Our perceived motivation will be analyzed and interpreted, perhaps misinterpreted. Rock's SCARF model makes us aware of the impact of our actions on interactions and helps us ease concerns people may not be aware of.

Do Try This At Home

Think of an important upcoming conversation. If you assume 100 per cent responsibility for the way you communicate and the way you are understood, how will you approach this discussion?

1. Who will you be talking with?
2. What will you be talking about?
3. What do you hope the other person will do as a result?
4. When and where will you talk?
5. What will be the best format? (formal/informal, group/one-to-one)
6. What facts are important to you?
7. What facts will be important to the other person or people?
8. What emotions or feelings might arise on your part or theirs?
9. How will the elements of the SCARF model affect them?
   - Status
   - Certainty
   - Autonomy
   - Relatedness
   - Fairness
10. What questions will you ask?
11. How will you know you are really listening?
12. What will you do if the need to be right arises for you?
13. What will you do if the need to be right arises for them?
14. How will you benefit from considering these issues?

Over the coming weeks, you can use these questions to help develop the habit of conscious, thoughtful planning for conversations that will enable you to assume 100 per cent responsibility for your communication and inspire the same accountability in others.

———••——

5

The Communication Styles

A week had passed since his first meeting with Emma. Paul had made little progress towards sorting out Project Delta. His first Thursday meeting with Burt had not gone well. He hadn't anticipated the degree to which Burt would be defensive.

Burt insisted his tried and true project management methods had worked around the world for many years. He didn't need help. He cited his successes with past projects. He was not responsible for the situation the team found itself in. Nobody, he argued, should be making him the scapegoat. The problem, according to Burt, was the programmers' incompetence and a general lack of discipline at Forthright.

It was a well-rehearsed monologue. Burt had made his position clear.

Paul had done his best to reassure Burt that his own role on the project was to focus on communication, teamwork and collaboration. He was there to be an additional resource, not to assign blame or diminish Burt's responsibility. He had tried to remember the SCARF principles, but his mind had gone blank after Status. Why hadn't he written them down? Status. Certainty. Autonomy. Relatedness. Fairness. He'd need to be better prepared, next time.

The Talk To Me Project, as he had begun to call it, along with his conversations with Katy and his approaching birthday, had led Paul to do more introspection than usual. For him, self-examination came with an unwelcome partner, self-doubt. As he rode the elevator to his office, he thought of his next meeting with his employees. He was better prepared than he had been for the previous week's fiasco. Could he recover?

He had examined his usual pattern of interaction with the group and was not pleased with what he found. Each communication looked like a variation of, "Here's the background. Here's the plan. Any questions?"

Communication was in one direction, from Paul to the others. He wasn't exactly giving orders, but he wasn't inviting a conversation, even though he asked for questions. The pattern was the same whether he was talking to one person or the group. He did the thinking. He decided on the actions. Others could ask questions – or not – and he preferred that they didn't. Was that part of what Emma had called the Lone Ranger behavior? It was no doubt related to the trait Katy had described as the need to be right.

He noticed that Tim Lee, his youngest and newest analyst, used a similar pattern. He'd state the problem, state the facts, and state his views. Though he got along well with Paul, Tim hadn't really begun to mesh with the other group members, something Paul had attributed to his status as the new kid in town. Perhaps there was something more going on?

For the upcoming meeting, he'd try to step out of his usual pattern and see what would happen. To assume 100 per cent accountability for the conversation, he would need to pay serious attention to how his messages would be received and understood, not just how he would send them. He'd also have to really listen to the others. And he'd have to consciously work to make his team feel safe in asking questions and raising issues. It sounded easy in theory, but what would it look like in real life?

He arrived at his desk and scribbled down some questions:

- What do they need to know? Want to know? Already know? Think they know?
- What do they say? Do? Hear? Ask? Want? Feel? Fear?
- What do I say? Do? Hear? Ask? Want? Feel? Fear?

He underlined the things he was usually aware of: what he thought people needed to know, what they said and did, and what he said and did. He noticed how much of the total picture he seldom considered. That he knew so little about his employees surprised him. No wonder they didn't seem to understand him; he didn't seem to be trying to understand them.

Paul had hesitated before writing the word "fear." He knew there was probably fear around, mostly the fear of looking stupid. But as he thought about it some more, he realized his team could also be afraid of being wrong, being judged, being misunderstood, being uncomfortable, and being vulnerable, not to mention that old familiar fear of the unknown. Misplaced or not, these fears were barriers to connection.

There was that word again, *connection*. It was the piece that seemed to be missing in these conversations and throughout all of Forthright. He tried to remember what it was like to be really connected in a conversation. What was going on when that happened?

The subject matter had to be interesting. Content was fundamental. But stuff had to be relevant too; conversations really flowed when they had some immediate application. It gave them context. Paul realized he always felt more comfortable when the person he was talking with seemed to care about him and his interests. They had a relationship, even if only one born from familiarity or arising from regular contact over time. Occasionally, as he had with Katy, he found he could have the same sort of easy conversation with a total stranger.

All these elements had something to do with connection. He sketched a diagram with three balls, Context, Content, and Contact. Where the three balls overlapped – perhaps that was where we make connection.

Paul saw, at once, that his focus was usually on the content of the conversation and mostly on his own message. If the other elements were there, it was by chance. He cared about his employees and assumed they knew that. But did they? What else was he assuming about them?

Paul knew he needed to do more asking and less telling. Just as he'd discussed with Katy, he'd have to be curious instead of being right.

The team was scheduled to meet in the conference room at 1:30. Lisa Firestone was early as always and seemed in a good mood. Kelly MacLeod and Tim Lee arrived together, followed by Tom Demitrios, who seemed uneasy. Rick Lavoie arrived a few minutes late, with apologies.

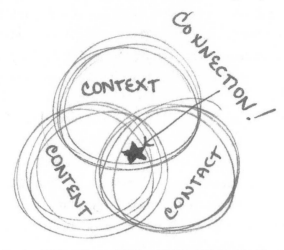

"Thanks for coming." Paul felt a weird sensation in his throat, like a hot ball. This was so uncomfortable. "I was wrong the other day. I owe you guys an apology."

Silence. People exchanged uneasy glances. Kelly fumbled for her mobile phone and turned it off. Rick stopped doodling.

"I blew it last week. I dropped a new, and pretty unusual program on you, without notice, and I didn't give anyone time to think it through or talk about it. I assumed that, because I understood the project, you would too. And when you didn't take to it, and I didn't know what to say, I blamed Emma Bateman. The part I forgot was that, when I heard about it, it hit me like a bomb. I had all weekend and a lot of conversations to adjust to the idea and I gave you what – five minutes? I was out of line and I am sorry."

There was a long silence. Paul resisted the urge to fill it. Painful.

Tom shuffled in his chair. "OK, while we're apologizing, I'll take a turn. I was out of line, too. That crack about fluffy work was uncalled for. I don't know where that outburst came from, but it won't happen again."

"It was hardly an outburst Tom." Lisa smiled at him. "You were expressing your feelings. It's probably fair to say we all had something going on. You just let it out. Personally, I was really confused. I still am."

"That makes two of us," Rick said.

"I'm guessing it makes six of us," said Paul. "So let's start again. Here's what I know."

Paul led them through the discussions with Emma and the information in her file about the need for better communication at Forthright. Everyone could find examples of what was wrong. Where was it going right?

Paul wrote a large question mark on his pad. How strange to need reminding to be curious. He was always curious about things, just not always curious about people. But once he remembered, the questions came easily. "How will that affect you?" "What will that mean?" "How important is that to you?" "Can you explain how you arrived at that conclusion?" "Can you tell us more about that?" A few times he asked, "How would that feel?" The group didn't seem ready for that one. To be honest, neither was he. Perhaps, with practice, they'd get used to discussing feelings. Feelings were going to be in the room, so they would need to acknowledge them.

As a group, they discussed Emma's rationale for asking a technical department to spearhead a project about human interaction. Eventually they agreed that, while they weren't experts, neither was anyone else at Forthright. However, they had research skills and unique access to the whole organization that others did not.

As for Emma's notion that conversation is a business tool, "that's a no-brainer," said Rick. "It's the process that starts every other process in this organization. Someone has to have an idea and then talk about it. It's how we get anything going. If we could get better at it, think of the time we'd save."

Paul drew them his Content/Context/Contact/Connect model. Tom suggested the elements could also be seen as sequential, not overlapping. Everyone took a turn at the white board. After 10 minutes, Tom looked at the mess on the board and said, "Maybe we don't have to settle this today. The point is to make sure they're all there."

They drew up a task list and chose assignments. They agreed to have checkpoint meetings every Friday, at 8:30. "And in between our primary mode of communication will be . . ." Rick paused as he beat a drum roll with the markers.

Several people replied in unison: "Conversations."

As they left the room, Rick was whistling the triumphant theme from *Rocky*. Get this right, Paul thought, and they would all be champions. He took the stairs, instead of the elevator, and headed to The Coffee Grounds. His team meeting had gone better than he'd expected and he was anxious to discuss it with Katy.

"I can see by your body language that your day went well," she said as he entered the shop. "Latte?"

"Am I that transparent?"

"Only on your birthday," she replied and presented a cupcake, complete with a lit candle.

"I'd nearly forgotten." He blew out the flame.

"You're only 45," said Katy. "Wait till you're my age. Then you'll really want to forget. What's up?"

Paul described his team meeting, how he had wanted to do something different after the fiasco of the previous week, and how the day's recovery effort had gone. "I had to remind myself to be curious but, once I got started, it wasn't too awful." He told Katy about his team, who they were, the comments they made, and their plans for moving forward. "We'll use my team to test the ideas as we develop them. We're both the experimenters and the lab rats."

"Good, safe environment for a prototype," Katy said. "Where else can you test the ideas?"

Paul thought for a second. "We absolutely have to use them for Project Delta. One of the reasons it's grinding on so slowly is that nobody's really talking to anyone else. It's all reports, whining and nagging. Someone from the marketing department, Lynnette Benson, has noticed the problem, too. She could be an ally in this. Aren't marketing people supposed to know something about communication? If we could get people to see how they talk to each other, it would be a good start towards better collaboration. At

TALK TO ME

the very least, having to pay attention to it will keep us awake during the meetings."

"Maybe you need more caffeine. I could send over a carafe or two. Speaking of giving you things, here's a birthday present." Katy handed him a small booklet, *Communication Styles – A Field Guide*, by Katy De Marco.

"Thanks. Looks like it could come in handy. Is this today's lesson?"

"How did you guess? You may have noticed that not everyone is like you. Sometimes that's a good thing. Sometimes it's a pain in the butt. Anyway, years and years of theory and research suggest that there are actually patterns in the ways we're all different. People tend to act in predictable ways, based on how they like to gather and process information."

"Yeah. Jenny, my wife, has a book about that. She used it to figure out how to handle her new boss."

"So you get the idea. Most of it comes out of the work of Carl Jung, he was a protégé of Freud's and …"

"Don't get all psychoanalytical. Having a coach is a big enough step for me." Paul laughed. He was only half joking.

"Don't worry. My point is that this theory has respectable roots. If I know my style and yours, I can predict areas where misunderstanding can creep into our relationship. If I'm smart, I'll figure out ways to avoid that. I've taken some of Jung's and his followers' ideas and put together this communication styles assessment to help people understand their own styles and spot other people's. There are four patterns: Guardians, Artisans, Idealists, and Rationals. The names actually date back to Plato."

"I think therefore I am?"

"That was Descartes. Plato said things like: 'Necessity is the mother of invention.' But that's not the point. The point is that this idea has been around a while."

Katy carried on. "Let's start with Rationals. They're big thinkers, driven by knowledge. They're also a small group, around 10 per cent of the population. They value logic and inventiveness. Being competent is huge for them. They're oriented towards the future. They're great goal setters, especially long-range goals, and they're strategic, big picture people. They don't always need evidence to support their ideas and they can go on intuition or gut feel. That can scare some other types. Their need to be right is strong and they can be competitive."

"Sounds like Tim Lee," Paul said.

"And probably other people you know. A lot of them find their way to systems work. Lots of CEOs too. Knowing even this much about Rationals, you can increase your communication success rate when you talk with them by focusing on ideas. Appeal to their intellect. Show that your ideas are both logical and creative. Ideas are good. Talk about the impact your ideas will have in the future. Paint the big picture; they don't need to see details right now. And Rationals don't care if your ideas are aligned with best practices in the industry; they want them to be good ideas."

Paul decided Emma must be a Rational. He might be one himself.

"Next we'll go with Idealists. I'm most familiar with them since I'm one of them. They're also about 10 per cent of the population. Identity drives them – their own and everyone else's. They want to help everyone to be their best, most authentic selves. Great teachers. They're empathetic, sometimes spookily so. They like harmonious relationships, want people to get along and will do just about anything to avoid conflict. They like to be inspired and are pretty good at inspiring others. Like the Rationals, they're future-oriented and make decisions from intuition, without a lot of facts. Their big weakness is that they can sometimes be too idealistic. And they often need everyone to love them. Know anyone like that?"

"You are describing Jenny, my lovely wife, the mind-reader and peacemaker. And I'll bet Lisa Firestone, on my team, is one. You're going to help me communicate better with Idealists?"

"Think about it. What's going to work for them?"

Paul thought of Jenny. "Well, you focus on people. They're not that interested in logic, certainly not the sort of logic I understand. You probably have to talk about feelings. And don't argue with them. They withdraw. Appeal to their high standards."

"Good. You're getting this," Katy said. "Idealists want to be inspired, so you need to be inspiring. Show that you feel something's important, but don't simply tell them. Be excited by the possibility. Arguing the case on the facts alone will not work with an Idealist. And don't throw numbers at them; they don't even hear them. Again, give them the big picture and show them how what you're talking about will improve the world."

"Improve the world? With Project Delta?"

"It doesn't have to lead to world peace, but if you want an Idealist to listen to you and your ideas, show them the intrinsic value, how it helps someone besides you."

"That's Jenny, for sure," said Paul.

"Now on to Guardians," Katy said. "Security drives them. They like predictability. They trust things that have worked for them in the past. They can be sticklers for procedures and following the rules. They believe evidence and usually need heaps of it to make a decision. They're great at sorting out and managing the details and are good administrators. You can usually rely on them to get a job done. Unfortunately, they can get caught up in process and be really bureaucratic. They're often pessimistic and they hate change. They're also about 40 per cent of the population."

"Burt Shepler," Paul said. "He's Mr. Process. And maybe Tom Demitrios, from my group. This is interesting and I think there's something to it. See if I'm getting this. These guys hate change, so we'll show them how what we propose won't be destabilizing. 'Evolution, not revolution,' and all that. Here's where we show up with an armload of facts. And they'll probably love best practices and success stories, since this means the idea worked before. Appeal to their sense of responsibility. They're also going to want to be sure every I and T is crossed and dotted."

"Dotted and crossed," Katy said. "I may be an Idealist, but I'm also a lawyer."

"Whatever, I guess I'm not a Guardian. What about the Artisans?"

"These people make up over 35 per cent of the population. Sensations drive them. They can do things spontaneously and are good at handling unexpected problems. They don't enjoy structure. They value timeliness and cleverness and that makes them resourceful and good at improvising. They're action-oriented, like to work fast, and more than any other type, they'll take risks. They live in the present and they're optimistic about the future, but they may leave things to chance, rather than plan. They also value freedom. Where they trip up is that they'll often choose short term tactics over long term strategy."

"That's Rick Lavoie. He's our go to guy when we're in a crunch, but I wouldn't want him planning the future. He doesn't seem to look more than five minutes ahead."

"So, how do you think we communicate with them?" Katy asked.

"Hmm. Let them know what has to happen right now and how they can be involved. I'm having trouble with this one."

Katy agreed. "Appeal to their need for excitement and stimulation. Do not be even the least bit boring. Show them what's bold and unconventional about your idea."

"What if there's a Guardian in the room?"

"Good point. Show the Artisan the idea is nifty and elegant. Show the Guardian how it's like something they know works. Here's another tip. Ask Rationals what they think. Ask Idealists what they feel. Ask Guardians what they've experienced. And ask Artisans how things look or sound to them."

"What type is Emma?"

"Ah! You'll have to figure that out for yourself. The important question is what type are you? The quiz is in the booklet. I'll get you another coffee. You'll be done before I get back."

What's Going On Here

As soon as Paul took on the Talk To Me project, he started paying attention to his own communication patterns. As often happens, the simple act of noticing his behavior began to change it. Awareness won't always spark change or even an intention to change. But change seldom comes without awareness. Developing a habit of examining your communication habits and the wants, needs and styles of those around you is the foundation for improvement.

Paul noticed that he didn't know what his employees thought, felt or understood because he didn't ask. Once he was aware of that, he had to remind himself to invite their participation and, over the course of the meeting, it became easier. When Paul began the meeting by admitting that he'd made a mistake, he gave everyone permission to be less than perfect. Acknowledging our humanity doesn't mean lowering our standards; it means moving one step closer to connecting with others at a human level, the level where real communication takes place.

Once we accept that it's OK to be human, we can recognize that not all humans are the same. Not everyone takes in, processes, and understands information the way we do. When people realize there are different communication styles, they no longer blame communication gaps on other people's bad intentions or incompetence.

Each of us has all the styles present to some degree; however, one style is usually dominant.

It's useful to be aware of styles that are different from our own. Knowing how to deliver messages that meet someone else's communication style increases the chances they will be interested in what you have to say and understand it. We can present information the way they like it. The more we can be flexible in our style, and adapt it to the style of the person we're talking to, the greater the chance of a conversational connection.

 Try This At Home

This short assessment will give you some clues about your communication style. There are no right or wrong answers and there is no one style that is better than the others. The goal is to provide you with some insight into your own communication style and that of others. Understanding communication styles can help you adjust your approach so you can connect with others on their wavelength.

Circle the answer that is most true for you.

1. I would rather be known for:
    - (a) Doing things properly
    - (b) Doing things brilliantly
    - (c) Doing things from the heart
    - (d) Doing things creatively

2. I feel good about myself when I:
    - (a) Am dependable
    - (b) Use my intelligence
    - (c) Relate well to others
    - (d) Am in action

3. I tend to trust:
    - (a) Tried and true methods
    - (b) Pure reason and logic
    - (c) My intuition
    - (d) My ingenuity

4. I'd like to have more:
    - (a) Certainty
    - (b) Efficient ways of doing things
    - (c) Self-awareness
    - (d) Adventure

5. I like to work with:
    - (a) Processes
    - (b) Ideas
    - (c) People
    - (d) Tools

6. My advice is:
    - (a) Be careful
    - (b) Be smart
    - (c) Be friendly
    - (d) Be flexible

7. I'd rather have:
   (a) Certainty
   (b) Knowledge
   (c) Wisdom
   (d) Spontaneity
8. My top strength is:
   (a) Reliability
   (b) Curiosity
   (c) Empathy
   (d) Creativity
9. The route to success is based on:
   (a) Following proven methods
   (b) Experimentation
   (c) An inspiring vision
   (d) Taking action
10. I'm most interested in:
   (a) Meeting my responsibilities
   (b) Solving problems
   (c) Possibilities for people
   (d) Making things work

Total the number of times you choose each letter

a =	b =	c =	d =	Total = 10
Guardian Style	Rational Style	Idealist Style	Artisan Style	

Note to readers: You can find the full text of Katy's booklet in Appendix Two. The assessment can be done, online, at http://talktomebook.com

If you're interested in a more in-depth look at your communication style, you may want to take an assessment such as the Myers-Briggs Type Inventory (MBTI). Learn more at http://itsunderstood.com/services/assessment/

———————

6

What's Going Right?

Paul hadn't been surprised to discover that his own Communication Style was Rational. The description in Katy's book was eerily accurate. His focus was always on ideas, the logical, intellectual approach. He was a big picture guy, not interested in detail. He trusted his hunches and he could always find a logical explanation to support them.

He could see where that might collide with other styles, especially Guardians, who like to see evidence and detail before making decisions.

Later that week, Paul shared Katy's booklet with his group and everyone did the communication styles assessment. As predicted, Lisa landed in the Idealist camp, Tim and Kelly showed up as Rational, Tom as a Guardian, and Rick rounded out the team as an Artisan. Paul had enjoyed witnessing their recognition of some essential truths about the way they communicated.

Lisa quickly noticed a need to adapt her style. "This tells me that I'll get through to you guys a whole lot better if I have either evidence or logic to back up my ideas instead of just passion and absolute conviction that something is the right thing to do. I have quite a bit of flexing to do."

To which Tom had responded, "And we'll stop rolling our eyes when you ask how something will affect people. It's not only your style; it's a question the rest of us don't naturally think of. I don't think we want you to give that up."

Tim had noticed the difference in the pace at which people process information. "What I get from this is that we who are "gut instinct" people need to recognize that half the department needs a lot more detail than we do. And they need more time to think about it."

Kelly added, "Half the department and half the world. I'd say the corporate style here at Forthright would lean towards Guardian, in spite of the whole maverick image."

The meeting had ended with a commitment to recognize the variety in communication styles and to flex their own approaches to meet other people's preferences. Then Rick added another point.

"If our communication style means we need something more – evidence, time, facts, feelings, whatever – so that we understand what the other person is saying, we should ask for it. I think that's the corollary to Paul's idea about being 100 per cent accountable. He talks about taking responsibility for making sure we are understood. I think each of us also can make sure we have what we need to understand, too. We all sit in meetings where nobody really understands what someone is talking about, but everyone pretends things are just fine. Nobody wants to ask a question and look stupid. How stupid is that?"

Paul walked to The Coffee Grounds thinking about Rick's idea. Questions are at the heart of learning and innovation. Yet so many people, including himself, would rather stay ignorant than look ignorant by asking a question. What was that about? And what could change it?

"You're right on time," Katy said. "I'll join you in a second."

Paul took his usual table. His sessions with Katy were becoming part of the rhythm of his life and he considered them time well spent. Money, too. Though Forthright was paying Katy's fee, he would gladly have paid it himself. Her perspective was valuable. He invariably left with a new idea and he always felt more confident about what he was doing after talking with her.

"So, what's up today?" Katy asked. "Did you try working with the communication styles?"

"We had a great discussion. We added a corollary to your 100 per cent responsibility idea."

"Cool. Tell me."

"We have to be accountable for how we understand as well as how we're understood. We can ask for the kind of information we need. You know how people go through meetings without asking for clarification because they don't want to look stupid. I've seen that. I've done it. What's with that?"

Katy returned the question. "What do you think?"

"It probably goes back to what we discussed in our first session – our need to be right. If we ask a question, it shows we don't have all the answers. So we don't ask. And we especially don't ask if the person is senior to us. So we just sit there and they get away with lousy communication. They probably think they're doing just fine."

"That reminds me of a story Emma once told me," Katy said. "Back in her days in the bank, she was at a meeting where a senior executive, thinking out loud, suggested an idea for a new product. It was a dumb idea, but it was coming from the guy in the corner office. So they invested time and money and developed the prototype and all the marketing jazz. They took the finished plan to the executive, for approval, expecting him to be delighted. What do you think he said?"

"Whose crazy idea was this?" Paul ventured.

"Something like that. It made quite an impact on Emma. Misunderstanding steps into the space where the unasked question should be. It can be costly. Now, I think she'd want to slap anyone who's confused by something she said and doesn't ask for what they need to get it clear."

"Thanks for the warning. I wonder if my employees just go along with my ideas." Paul paused. "Never mind. I know the answer. That's something else we can talk about as a group. We could spend so much time talking about how we talk to each other that we'll never do anything. That's not the point of this exercise."

"Think about it in terms of your world. If this were a computer system, there's a big flurry of activity when you develop it and lots of action around implementation, but once you've rolled it out, what's going on?"

"Monitoring, maintenance and thinking about improvements for the next release. I see what you mean. We're in the development phase."

"So how's the Talk To Me project going?"

"Well, research from inside and outside Forthright tells us managers think they're communicating well enough overall, yet employees disagree. When we ask managers what the problems are, it boils down to not enough time, not enough information, and too many meetings."

"So you're starting with the problems?" Katy asked.

"Yeah. Communication's not working. What's wrong with it? What's causing that? What do we do about it?"

"That's one way to approach it. What might be another?"

Paul thought for a second. "Well, ignoring the problem won't get us anywhere. I guess we could look at what's working. We've started examining exit interviews and focus group feedback to find departments where there seems to be good communication. We haven't got too far with that, yet."

"If you look for problems, what are you going to find?"

"Problems, more problems – and maybe a solution."

"If you look for what's going well, what will you find?"

"A needle in a haystack?" Paul checked to see how his joke landed. "Don't hit me, Katy, I get it. You get more of what you focus on. I've seen this. Sometimes we get user feedback surveys that tell us 95 per cent of people are satisfied. Who do we focus on? The dissatisfied five per cent. Next thing we know, only 90 per cent of our users are satisfied. We got so focused on fixing the problems, we let go of the good stuff."

"There's always something that works," said Katy. "Building on that gives you an alternative to looking for problems. Being positive is a whole lot more fun, easier on our stress levels and, frankly, it works better. Do you know anything about Appreciative Inquiry?"

"I think I read an article about it. They used it in the US Army or somewhere. They look at the good stuff going on in an organization and try to make more of it?"

"It was the Navy," Katy said, "but you remembered the main point. It's a process for introducing change that asks, 'What's working?' instead of, 'What's wrong here?' You look at the organization with an appreciative eye instead of a critical one. Ideally, the whole organization is involved, though you can start anywhere. You get people to tell stories about times things were really working. Then you have them talk about what was going on around them, what the circumstances were. You try to create the circumstances that prevailed when people and the organization were at their best. Then you build from there."

"Isn't that going to keep you stuck in the past?" Paul asked.

"Good question. Remember that article about the human brain not liking change?"

"Yeah. The brain can't tell the difference between change that's dangerous and change that's just different. Any change looks threatening, so we resist it."

"Exactly! Appreciative Inquiry – AI for short – helps you bring the best parts of the past with you into the future. It lets you know you can do this new thing because you're using some old reliable and transferable skills you've used before. It makes change less threatening."

"Does it work with Guardians? They're anchored in the past, wary of change and trust the tried and true."

"Done well, AI can work with anyone. But, yes, Guardians respond well to being reminded about things that worked well in the past and how what you propose is a bit like that. Why do you ask?"

"I'm meeting with Burt Shepler tomorrow, and I need a strategy. Our meeting last week was about me listening to him tell me how great he is and how much he doesn't need help. I think he leans towards Guardian when he's not just being a controlling jerk. He won't enjoy having me try to help him build communication and collaboration. He made that pretty clear. I'm sure he thinks I have nothing to offer. If I think about SCARF, he'll be stressed on all counts. He'll go along with it because Emma's driving this. His management style is: Kiss Ass Upward, Kick Ass Downward."

"Is that true?"

"Maybe not precisely, but he's nobody's dream date."

"Can you think of him as a learning opportunity? You know how they say when the student is ready the teacher appears. You can try out what you're learning about communication on Burt. You have to work with the guy anyway."

"Not sure the theory works on people like Burt, but I'll try anything. If these ideas work with him, they'll probably work anywhere. You know, like the song about New York, 'If I can make it there, I'll make it anywhere'?"

Katy laughed. "How are you planning to approach the conversation?"

"He's going to be uncomfortable and may be defensive. If I'm going to connect with him at all, I'll have to neutralize some of that. I'll refresh on that SCARF model tonight. My thought is that Relatedness is probably the place that offers the most hope. We both want this project to succeed. That's some common ground and a shared goal. Certainty and Autonomy can be addressed by developing some clarity around what's going to happen and who's going to do what. Can't do much about status, since he'll see me as representing the CEO. And Fairness? The whole Project Delta isn't fair."

"Good start," Katy said. "If Burt feels he gets as much as he gives, that can balance Fairness."

"What does he get from me? He's got to share his precious Project Manager role."

"What do you have that he needs?"

Paul had stopped being annoyed when Katy turned his questions back on him and made him think. "Helping him get the project back on track and implemented?"

"That's big. Anything else?"

"Saving his project, his job and his butt's not enough?"

"Could you help him learn to communicate better? I'm serious. You could do it."

"And where's your Florida swampland? I'm more likely to buy that." What was the woman thinking? "I'll save his butt first. Let's get back to that appreciative thing."

"I'm no expert, though I've read a bit. The Appreciative Inquiry process isn't complicated. You identify an area where you want to be great. You have appreciative discussions about the best of what is. Then, as a group, you envision what could be, decide what should be and then create what will be. Discover, Dream, Design and Deliver – I think those are the terms."

"I can't use a word like dream around Burt," Paul said. "Not just him. Words like that make people nervous."

"Do words like that make you nervous?"

Paul let his silence answer.

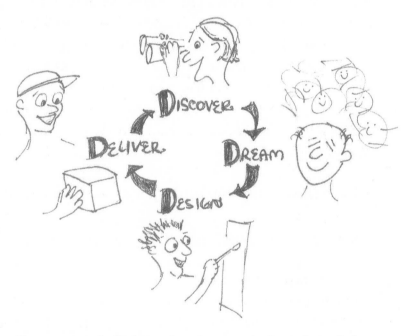

Katy continued. "It has to be a big stretch. Does *desire* feel as powerful? Words shape how we think and feel about something, and thoughts and feelings drive our action. I'd stick with *dream* unless it was going to scuttle the deal. An assumption of the AI process is that the words we use are powerful. They have their own energy and shape how we feel and think about the things they describe."

"I'll try it on. But if Burt chokes, we'll retreat and make it *desire*. Fair?"

Katy nodded. "Back to my oversimplified version of AI. The very act of asking questions influences the group. Appreciative questions touch something special, authentic and heartfelt and, when that's expressed, the group changes. You start by having people tell stories about a time when the issue you're exploring went well. Then you ask them what was going on, what they valued and how they contributed. When the stories are gathered, patterns emerge that reflect a bigger picture, a shared impression that lots of people can relate to. You describe what might be possible and, because you grounded it in real experience, people can see that it is possible. You build the new reality from there. There's a lot more to it, of course."

"That's interesting, and it may be useful," Paul said. "I like the focus on what's possible. If you concentrate on problems, you're always in Fix It Mode. If you focus on possibility, you're almost guaranteed to be more creative and innovative. And you won't be depressed. Hanging around my wife, I've learned being positive can be contagious. You don't pretend there are no problems, but you look for what will get you to a good place rather than what got you to a bad place. We get on the bus that's going somewhere, not the one that's going for repairs."

"Nice image."

"I also like that the US Army uses it. Gets away from any sort of fluffy, soft skills image."

"It's the Navy."

"Whatever. I'll check out this AI stuff. In the meantime we'll step up the hunt for strengths. We already know where the problems are. We've known for years and it hasn't helped. Thanks, Katy."

What's Going On Here ?

Paul's decision to focus on the positive aspects of communication at Forthright represents a major shift in perspective. It will alter the way he thinks about his work and will influence the way others view their work and participate in the organization.

Remembering times when we felt productive, connected, inspired, and excited about our work doesn't automatically make us productive, connected, inspired, and excited; however, it does remind us that being that way is possible. After all, it's our own experience. It introduces the possibility that we could do it again.

Looking at problems, determining their causes, and trying to fix them are standard operating procedure in organizations around the globe. Many of us approach our personal lives that way, too. In recent years, however, some organizations have begun to focus on using strengths and building on what is working, instead of fixing what's broken or working on flaws and weaknesses. The Appreciative Inquiry movement, work around Emotional Intelligence, the emergence of positive psychology, with its focus on wellness and successful performance, the rise of personal and executive coaching, and the ideas that appear in books such as *Now Discover Your Strengths*, *Learned Optimism* and *The Art Of Possibility* have helped thousands of people make that shift. (see Appendix IV – Learn More)

When you begin to ask appreciative questions in an organization in which it's fashionable to be cynical, you can expect some smart remarks and an invitation to take off the rose-colored glasses. Still, even in groups and organizations where pessimism seems to have taken root, people can usually recall something positive, some strength or some experience that stands out as an example of something good.

It takes time to develop an appreciative eye, so trained are we by our society to look for imperfection. You can speed up the process by engaging a partner or several colleagues to start practicing what we might call *Appreciative Communication,* asking appreciative questions and seeing the organization from a strengths-based perspective, looking for possibilities instead of looking for flaws and trouble.

 **Try This At Home**

This exercise invites you to sample some appreciative questions. In answering them, you'll gain a sense of the approach and the process. You may also observe that something happens to you as you recall high points, those times when you and your group or organization were at your best.

- What drew you to the topic of workplace conversations?
- What ideas do you have for ways a communication initiative might help your group or organization achieve its mission or goals?
- When you look at your group or organization with an appreciative eye, what positive characteristics show up, in its daily life and service to others, when it is at its best?
- What positive characteristics contribute to your group or organization's capacity for co-operation and collaboration?
- What strengths in your group or organization help you operate at your best?
- What do you want more of in your group or organization?
- If you had three wishes, what would you wish for your group?
- How might appreciative communication help you realize these wishes?
- Can you describe the ways appreciative communication contributes to success in your group or organization?
- How do people in your group or organization benefit from hearing and telling stories of times when it and they were at their best?
- Are there situations in which you find yourself where you can practice asking positive questions?
- What questions might you ask to elicit positive stories?

———

CHAPTER

7

I Want That, Too!

On Thursday morning, Paul headed for the conference room, silently reciting his new mantras:

"Keep things positive."

"Find the common ground."

"Don't discount the past."

"Communicate with style."

He couldn't decide if he was dreading his meeting with Burt or looking forward to it. Although it would be a difficult conversation, he felt prepared. He should; he'd been rehearsing it since the previous week's disastrous effort.

Paul had gone into that meeting certain he could win Burt's agreement using logic. Their CEO believed that adding Paul to the project management team was putting additional skills where they were needed. So did Paul. His only role was to focus on and improve communication and teamwork. But Burt saw Paul's assignment as unnecessary interference. He'd made that clear.

Logic had told Paul that Burt would welcome some help. Burt's reaction told him something else. He'd read – and doubted – that emotion is at work in all decisions, even when we think it's not. We retrofit the logic to

TALK TO ME

suit our decisions. Could there be some truth in that idea? If so, what was Burt feeling about this?

He'd never thought about Burt's feelings before. Simply noticing his own feelings was new for Paul. Burt didn't seem like a feelings kind of guy. Even so, Paul had to recognize that everyone had feelings, didn't they?

He'd feel threatened. Emma, his boss of bosses, was behind this change. He'd likely assume she didn't have confidence in him. Would he lose his job? He'd been hired, specifically, to manage Project Delta.

Perhaps he'd feel his competence was in question. That would be a serious issue for someone like Burt, so quick to remind everyone of his track record and his certifications. He certainly had what Katy had described as the need to be right. Paul was struggling with that himself.

Though he might not be conscious of it, Burt's brain would interpret the change as a threat to his status, both in the company and as a professional. Paul's favorite article from Emma's file, the one about SCARF, had told him threats to status are as real to the brain as physical pain. He hadn't devised a way to ease that stress for Burt. But he could make sure not to mention Emma, or blame her for the situation.

He'd have to work on the other elements. What were they?

Certainty. Burt was a process oriented guy. Paul had put a short document together that outlined who would do what and, to the extent possible, when. He could tick off the Certainty box.

Autonomy. Having to share project responsibility with Paul would put that out of balance for Burt. Could defining and distinguishing their roles rebalance the situation?

Relatedness. Would it help Burt to know that Paul wanted the same result he did? They both wanted Project Delta complete, implemented, and working. How could he make that clear? Burt would want some evidence that Paul was on his side.

Fairness. Who were they kidding? Nothing was fair. Paul had to chuckle, as he recalled his dad's frequent refrain, "When you start thinking life isn't fair, stop. Start thinking of a way to make it fun." Putting the words "fun" and "fair" in the same breath as "Project Delta" was ridiculous. But

Katy had suggested fairness was about a balanced exchange, so Burt would surely get something valuable out of this. How about a successful implementation? If Burt learned something, that would be a bonus.

Paul wasn't sure of Burt's communication style. His love of process and apparent shortage of empathy ruled out Artisan and Idealist. Burt seemed mostly Guardian with a dollop of Rational. Paul would prepare for both. Both styles valued logic and that was on his side. The Talk To Me project was looking for solutions to problems. That would appeal to a Rational. And it was looking for processes to make those solutions happen. That would appeal to a Guardian. He was well-equipped with data and facts so loved by Guardians.

He'd try to demonstrate respect for Burt's competence and knowledge, important to someone with the Rational style; and he'd need to show appreciation for his work, something needed by a Guardian.

Paul was a few minutes early when he arrived at the meeting room with a coffee for each of them. Burt was already standing by the window.

"This is the room where I had my first job interview at Forthright," he said.

Paul resisted an impulse to make a joke about revisiting the scene of the crime.

"How long has it been? A year?"

"Close to it. The time's gone fast. It's hard to believe."

"Well they say time flies when you're having a good time."

Burt took a seat. "Then we'd better get the fun started."

Rather than facing Burt, as he had the week before, Paul sat beside him. It seemed a collaborative stance, rather than confrontational. "I thought it would help me, and maybe you, if we had a bit of structure for how we're going to handle the communication on this project. I'd like to know your thoughts. To get us started, I've put a framework together."

Paul produced his planning document just as Burt pulled a flow chart from his file. "Me too," said Burt.

The headings on Paul's list and the boxes on Burt's chart were almost the same. They related to meetings, reports and people. Paul had labeled the last cluster culture. Burt had called it morale and depicted it as a band running below the chart.

"Well," said Burt, "there's no argument about what's important."

Paul was relieved. Maybe this meeting wouldn't be so bad. "We're agreed on the headings. Let's look at details. We've both listed meetings first. What's your idea of a good meeting? The sort you dream of?" Oh, no. Had he just used the word *dream* with Burt Shepler?

"The right people are in the room – a dream team of people who need to be there, not a cast of thousands. And they're not people who have to go back and check with their bosses, who then have to check with their bosses. They're people who can make decisions."

"Have you ever been on a project where the meetings were like that, with the right people who can make decisions?" asked Paul.

Burt hesitated. "Not lately. But I have led big projects where everyone was authorized to make decisions."

"At the bank?"

"No, at HAL. I don't think it was a more trusting environment, but people had – or maybe they just took – more responsibility for making decisions. It's different when you're the vendor. Your clients are external. You meet their deadlines or lose the business. It's not only the sales force that recognizes that."

"So, if we look at Delta, do you think our people don't fully under-stand the business reasons for the project?" Paul recalled the project kick-off meeting. It had been the full package, T-shirts, balloons and hoopla. "Wasn't it communicated at the project launch meeting?"

"It was, and we thought that would be enough to motivate people. It looks like it wasn't. Now that we're talking about it, I think one of our prob-lems on this project is a lack of urgency. It relates to not really grasping why we're doing it."

"Maybe we could use some sort of urgency and purpose refresher," Paul said. "The other day Lynnette showed me what the people in the field have to do to process a transaction while they wait for us to deliver. Even I was amazed at how clunky that workaround is. That raised my sense of urgency.

Could we bring a few real users into a meeting to show us what they do? If everyone sees and feels their pain, it might be a little more inspiring than what we've got now."

"Which is Lynnette harping about the date. We are all quite aware we're late. Nagging doesn't help."

"I know. I used to tune her out, myself. But imagine yourself in her shoes, Burt. She's hearing complaints from the field, her group is funding the project at something like nine grand a day, and they still don't know when the thing will be ready. You don't have to be particularly empathetic to see why she's upset."

"She's not the only one frustrated by the lack of progress." Burt shifted uncomfortably in his chair. "How do you think I feel? I'm the project manager – and the favorite candidate for scapegoat. But I'm doing everything I can to control this mob."

"Are you trying to control the right things?"

"I'm trying to control anything I can. But, to use an overworked expression, it's like herding cats."

"Could you be trying too hard? My experience with cats is that, when you ignore them, they come to you. Not that you should ignore people in these meetings." What was he saying? His mind was not connecting with his mouth. What would Katy say if she were here? "Can I make an observation? What I've seen is that you're trying to control the meetings during the meetings. Could there be a better time to exert control?"

"A better time?" Burt looked puzzled. "Like, before the meeting? I'd love it if people could be better prepared. But I can't control that."

Paul thought of how he usually prepared for the meetings – he skimmed the long and confusing status reports. "Maybe people aren't prepared for meetings and can't make decisions because they can't find the information they need in the status reports."

"As you may recall, the reports started out simply. Various people asked us to add things. I think we even added new fields for you."

"Guilty as charged." Ouch! Why had he raised that issue?

"Maybe we need to take a look at the status reports. Highlight the important stuff. Relegate the arcane to the back page. That could be a start. If they're shorter, and clearer, and faster to read, people might use them better."

Burt committed to working with his assistant Tara to streamline the reports. He felt they could have a draft to discuss the following week.

"I think we're doing well, Burt. Let's say we have these new reports and people like and use them, what do you want to happen at the meetings? What's a good outcome, for you?"

"Decisions about next steps. I'd love to hear less about what's already happened and more about what's happening next."

"I want that, too. Right now, we don't have discussions; we have a string of reports. As I see it, there are two kinds of discussions: discussions to discover something and discussions to decide something. When we spend so much time on the first, we don't get to the second."

"So, what do you suggest?" Burt asked.

"Let's go back to controlling what happens before the meeting; maybe you control the agenda, rather than the meeting. Advertise the decisions that need to be made. Make the meeting about deciding rather than re-porting. We need decisions on this, this, and this. People need to come ready to approve an idea or improve it."

"Approve or improve. I like that. That'll make them do their homework. Or will it?"

Paul wasn't sure. "It's worth a try. What we're doing now isn't getting either of us what we want. If the meetings have a clear intention, people will pay attention."

"Approve or improve. Intention or attention. Nice slogans. Are you try-ing out for a job in Marketing?"

"Very funny. I have no ambition in that direction. Still, this Talk To Me business is opening up my eyes – or my ears or mind or something. Being conscious of how we talk to each other is new for me. We all think we can talk, since we've been doing it since we were babies. But we take it for granted that people understand us. There's actually more to it than just opening your mouth."

"And, in my case, often putting your foot in it," Burt said. "I'll admit that, when I heard about your project, I thought it was pretty strange. Still do. All that soft skills stuff is so unpredictable. Way outside my box."

"It's not in the Project Manager Book of Knowledge?"

"Not the last time I looked. Maybe it should be."

"It's not really so far out of the project manager's world if we think of communication as a process, instead of an event."

"Hmm. I'll confess to a bias for process," Burt said, "though not process for the sake of process, like we had at the bank. I took the job here to get away from that. Forthright's smaller than the bank, and it has this reputation for doing things in a nimble way. I was attracted by the idea that there might be a bit of breathing room for projects. We'd get work done, instead of filling out forms."

"And now that you're here?"

"I don't miss the forms about forms and the checkers checking the checkers. I hate to admit it, but I kind of miss the structure. I'd like to feel things were more in control."

"And when you feel things are out of control, what do you do?"

"Hah! I get it. I try to control anything I can, including the wrong things."

"Will our new approach to meetings help you prevent that?"

"Maybe. I can't control the outcome, but I can control the input. It's too late to make the big changes for tomorrow's meeting. We'll get it set up for next week."

What's Going On Here ?

Paul's role was to help Burt get Project Delta back on track. If Burt and Paul were to look at the situation from a purely logical perspective, there is little to worry about:

- Their CEO has requested the move.
- Burt can use some help in a difficult project.
- Paul has skills that could be applied to the situation.
- Paul is already known, liked and respected by the rest of the team.

But even the most intellectually gifted people among us are highly influenced by emotion. As neuroscientists explore and understand the structure and function of the amazing human brain, they describe a brain that thinks, the prefrontal cortex, that is wrapped around an emotional brain, the limbic system. The emotional brain is sometimes referred to as the *lizard brain* or *reptilian brain* because even primitive animals have this type of brain. Its purpose is to keep us alive.

One of several organs of the limbic system is the amygdala, a danger sensor that scans the environment for threats. When it senses danger, it shoots first and asks questions later. It produces a state known as an *emotional hijack*. Blood flows to the large muscles in the legs. Breath becomes quick and shallow. Functions like digestion slow down. The thinking brain shuts down. All energy is directed towards survival. The body prepares to fight, flee, or freeze.

This reaction saved our species in early times. Today, however, it can be inconvenient. The amygdala, skilled at noticing shifts in the normal pattern of things, perceives all change as danger. When we're stressed, it's preparing the fight or flight reaction, and temporarily shuts down the thinking brain. (You may recall a time when you emerged from a stressful conversation in which you said something that made you wonder, "What was I thinking?" You probably weren't thinking. Your amygdala prevented it.)

Both Paul and Burt are intelligent men, yet neither is emotionally aware. Both will benefit from recognizing and naming their feelings and from learning about emotional intelligence.

Whether or not he recognizes it, Burt will have an emotional reaction to the situation. This will cause him stress, impair his judgment, and make the conversation difficult. Paul knows this. He calls on empathy as he tries to anticipate what Burt will be feeling so he can drive some of the stress out of the conversation.

Paul is also emotionally invested. His first attempt at a dialogue with Burt went badly and he doesn't want to repeat the experience. He needs to stay calm and positive. Preparation helps. Fortunately, Burt also seems to want a better outcome this time. And he is prepared as well.

Each of them has come to the meeting with his thoughts prepared and documented. They've identified the same topics as being important. Had that not been the case, they would need discussion to reveal what was important and together, they could build a list that worked for both.

In this conversation, it doesn't take long to establish that Paul and Burt want the same thing. They share a dream. Stress is reduced when we know someone wants the same results we do, especially on an important issue. The sooner you can establish that you share objectives, the sooner the real conversation can begin. You have something that relates you and are more likely to collaborate than merely co-operate.

Paul's questions about the desired outcome of the Delta meetings do more than build relatedness. They also help Burt to focus on what's really important. When you are clear about your goal, you are more likely to reach it. Once Burt realized that what he wanted from the meetings were decisions about the future, the process of reporting past events during the meeting looked dispensable. It was, in fact, something that could be handled through a better pre-meeting reporting process.

Try This At Home

Think of a situation happening or brewing where you work or live. This exercise will have you look at the parties, including you, and what's at stake, emotionally, for each.

1. What do you think is at stake for you?
2. What is the feeling that goes with that?
3. What is the best outcome for you?

4. Imagine you're one of the others involved. What's at stake for them?

5. What do you think they might be feeling about that?

6. What is the best outcome for that other person?

7. Where do your best outcome and theirs overlap? This is the common ground – and the place from which you can build the conversation.

8. How can you help the other person understand that you share their goal?

———•◆•———

8

Not Another Re-plan

here was a chill in the air as Paul crossed the parking lot. Fall was coming, for sure. He was almost looking forward to the Project Delta meeting. Would Burt remember his commitment to communicate consciously? Perhaps Burt wasn't such a bad sort, after all.

He arrived in the meeting room, right on time, to find Taylor Flynn, who led the programmers, and Tara O'Sullivan, Burt's assistant, deep in conversation – a worried conversation, judging by their expressions. They didn't seem to notice his entrance. Paul flipped through the bundle of reports Tara had carefully prepared, as she did for every meeting. Taylor's report was missing. Perhaps that explained his huddle with Tara.

The rest of the group straggled in. Burt fiddled with the projector. Lou Amyot, from Finance, checked his email. Belle Hinson, one of the auditors, was setting up her laptop. She always took notes. At least, that's what she said. Paul imagined she was really writing her memoirs. Lynnette Benson arrived and sat next to Paul.

"How's it going?" Paul asked her.

"Better than the last time we talked, except for this weekly ordeal. Next week I may bring Ron along, just so he'll believe my stories about how bad it is. I'm sure he thinks I'm making it up. I also think he must wonder if I'm pulling my weight on this team. Sometimes I wonder, myself."

Ron Walters was Lynnette's boss, the senior VP of Marketing. He likely knew how bad the meetings were. They were famous throughout Forthright.

"Pulling your weight? What more can you do?" Paul said.

"Some days, I wish we could just pull the funding and cancel the project."

"Could you? Would you?"

"Probably not. Too much already invested. I'm just so tired of waiting and nagging and waiting and nagging."

Burt cleared his throat and threw them a disapproving glance. "Can we get started?" He switched on the slide show.

The meeting followed the usual script. Against the soundtrack of Tara's and Belle's keyboards, the reports revealed little progress. Eyes glazed over. Tara had stopped dimming the lights for the slideshow five weeks earlier, after Lou had fallen asleep. That led Burt to change the clip art in his slides, but it was the same plot.

Taylor was the last to report. "As I've been telling you since the start of this project, the work we're doing isn't simple. Plus, we're short-handed because of the holidays, some staff turnover, and Svetlana Jidenko's maternity leave."

Paul could hear Lynnette's sharp intake of breath.

Taylor continued. "I think, as a group, we may have underestimated the technological challenge. We're really breaking new ground. We're going to need everyone's support here."

After another minute of what Paul heard as, "Blah blah blah," Taylor announced a seven week delay in delivering the code to the testing group. "Maybe six weeks, but I'm saying seven, just to be on the safe side."

Tara had stopped typing. Lou was working his calculator. Belle rolled her eyes. Paul looked at Lynnette to see if she was still breathing.

All eyes turned to Burt. "A seven week delay and we are only hearing about it now?" Burt was turning red. "You are supposed to let me know these things as soon as they come to light. How am I supposed to explain this to the Management Committee? I can't, I won't, go to them with news of another delay. I've been assuring them all was under control."

Taylor was ready with his defense. "At every single meeting of this group, I've been talking about the difficulties we're having. You knew that would impact the schedule. I was waving this big red flag and nobody ever seemed concerned – or even interested."

Paul couldn't recall having witnessed anything that resembled a red flag. Taylor had come to the meeting every week complaining of something or other. If he'd included a warning about the date slipping, it had been so deeply buried in his *poor me* story that it was no surprise that nobody caught it.

"You never told us this would lead to delays," said Belle. "You're always complaining about something. The sky is always falling. How are we supposed to know when it's true?"

"I have been telling you for weeks," Taylor replied. "I can't be responsible if you people never listen."

Paul's recent reading had told him about the danger of using the sweeping generalizations *you always* and *you never*. They make people defensive. Belle had used both phrases in one breath and Taylor had, predictably, defended. And what about Taylor? Didn't he recognize his own responsibility to communicate so he would be understood?

"What's the running cost on this project?" Lou asked, though he knew the answer. "Nine thousand a day? For seven weeks? That's $315,000. We're already well over budget. This is not good."

"And that's not including the cost of the time we're spending in these meetings and the work we're all doing behind the scenes," Belle said. "It's probably double that."

"We miscalculated," said Taylor. "When we started the project we used the best information we had about the system we're buying and what the users needed to do with it. Reality wasn't quite the same. Plus Audit kept adding new tracking requirements."

"Wait one minute," said Belle. "I asked if you could include them without any trouble. You gave me this big smile and said, 'Piece of cake!' Tara you were there, you remember. There's no way tracking was presented as a requirement. Don't try to blame us for your delay."

"If they weren't requirements, they should have been," said Lou. "Tracking is a critical issue; we're not introducing this project for our amusement. We need to show value."

"Let's not shoot the messenger," Taylor said. "We simply have to re-work the plan. We'll manage."

Lynnette stiffened. Paul could see that she was shaking. "Did I hear that right? We simply have to re-work the plan? Is that the only consequence of this? A new plan? What about the people in the field? A year ago, we told them we were going to give them a system that would improve transaction entry and give them better customer information. Ten months ago this team started working on it. This isn't about making their work easier; it's about making it possible. It's about offering products and services customers are demanding. It's about making money for this organization. It's about paying all our salaries."

She stood up. "These people are our sales force. If they don't meet their targets, there are consequences. Real consequences. They feel it in their paycheck. Their families feel it. They don't get to say, 'We have to re-work the plan.' They don't get to blame Belle and her tracking system, or the testers or the documentation people, or Lana Jidenko and her baby."

Lynnette had stopped shaking and was now at the whiteboard, where she printed: No Consequences. "That's our problem," she said. "There are no negative consequences. There are no positive consequences, either. We've all been sitting here for half a year, thinking, 'Well, I've done my bit.' But have we? If we have, then why isn't Delta up and running?"

Lynnette looked at Burt, who avoided making eye contact. Her pause, perhaps two seconds, seemed to last forever.

"The point of creating this team was to put all our brains and hearts in the same room and work together. Our hearts aren't in this. I don't even think our brains are in it. We're not working together. We're not doing anything together. We barely even talk to each other."

With those words, Lynnette handed Paul an opportunity he hadn't known he was looking for. Could he take his ideas about conversation and apply them to a real situation? They were just ideas, some only half formed.

This was the sort of mess the Talk To Me project was designed to work with or prevent. But he wasn't ready. He didn't have all the answers.

"Lynnette," he said, and at once he felt that familiar discomfort heating his throat. "Can you tell me about a time, when you felt you were part of a team whose hearts and minds were in the project – when you felt people really were working together for a common goal?"

Lynette looked at him as if he had just arrived from Jupiter. "I beg your pardon?"

"I'd like to hear about a time when you worked with a team under what you might consider ideal circumstances. It could help us to know what good performance looks like."

"Oh, get serious!" Belle slapped her laptop closed to make it clear she wasn't interested. "We're months late and way over budget and we're going to have a gab-a-thon about pie in the sky? I've got better things to do."

"Come on, Belle," Lou said. "I'd like to hear what Lynnette has to say. We're here anyway. It can't make things any worse. I don't know where Paul's going with this, but I'm willing to tag along. I know that Emma's got his team researching communication. She's worried and frankly, so are the rest of us on the Management Committee. We've slid into some really bad habits. We don't listen. We don't show respect. Today's a good example. I also think we need to pay some attention to what Lynnette said about consequences. Burt, it's your meeting. What do you think?"

Burt looked at Paul. "Actually, it's our meeting. We're booked till 4:30 anyway. Let's see what Paul has up his sleeve. I'm about ready to try anything. He can bring in a Ouija board if he likes, or the Sugarplum Fairy. What we've been doing hasn't worked."

"I hear the Sugarplum Fairy is busy," Belle said, "but the Tooth Fairy may be available if we book now."

Tara, who rarely spoke in these meetings, stepped in. "Belle, be nice. We all want to see this thing move ahead and give the people in the field what they need before we all die of old age. Let's give Paul a chance."

Belle sat back, arms folded. "OK, let's see what fairy story Lynnette can dream up."

Paul joined Lynnette at the whiteboard. "Tell me about a time when you were on a team that really worked well together."

"OK, though I'm not sure what good it will do. What comes to mind is the Pinnacle project. It was my first project here at Forthright. Some of the people in this room were on the team. What made it special for me was that the work felt important. We had a very clear idea what we were doing and who we were doing it for – the new employees. Since we've all been a new employee, we could relate to them. It was a technically challenging project too, so there was a whiff of adventure about that aspect of it. We played up the mountain climbing angle. I thought that was kind of silly, at the time, but it turned out to be a good metaphor."

"How did you feel?" Paul asked. "How did you perform?"

"I worked pretty long hours. Everyone did. But it seemed worthwhile. The meetings were fun and productive. When someone had a setback, they asked for help, and they got it. We'd have done just about anything for each other."

Nikki Chan, who had also been on the Pinnacle project, was nodding vigorously.

"We got to know each other, as people, not just colleagues," Lynnette continued. "Again, that's something I didn't really think was important. I try to be all business. But it was useful to know where people were coming from, what their quirks were, especially when things got really busy. I did some work I'm really proud of. We all worked hard not to let the team down."

Paul looked at the list he'd made while Lynnette was talking.

- Clear objectives.
- Knew audience.
- Adventure. Metaphor.
- Colleagues as people.
- Quirks.
- Mutual support.

"Great, Lynnette. Thanks." He turned to Lou. "Want to take a turn?"

"Sure. Does it have to be work related?"

"Not necessarily. It's about working together."

"OK. My best team experience was sailboat racing. The boat was called "Balance Sheet." We had a team of five, all accountants. We had the same people for three seasons, all with a few years' experience. We determined at the first team meeting over beers at the clubhouse that the goal was to have fun and sail well. We had a good first season and improved from there. You'll like this Paul – one of the things we did was analyze communication during the race. We examined who needed to talk to whom about what and when. As I recall, doing that one exercise moved us up five places in the fleet standings. What stood out for me was that everyone knew his or her job and did it. And we let people do their jobs. Unlike other boats in the fleet, there was no yelling. It was a calm boat."

"And just where are we sailing? I'm starting to drift off," Belle muttered.

"Where that ties in with what Lynnette said about Pinnacle is that we all had clear expectations. And we all had the same expectations. We understood our roles and we knew we could rely on each other to do the job. We enjoyed each other as people. I was proud to be a member of that team. I remember using some of the things we learned on the boat with my group, here in Finance. I'd forgotten about that."

Still at the white board, Paul had added items to his list.

- Did jobs
- No interference
- Shared expectations
- Knew roles
- Communication patterns
- Pride
- No yelling

"OK," he said. "If I were to go around the room and ask every one of you what a great group working experience looks like – we could do that at a separate session – we'd have a good list of what's important to us as a group. Many of the same characteristics will be repeated from team to team. Lynnette's and Lou's stories described very different situations, but they had a lot in common, especially around shared objectives, communication, and regard for people as people."

"So how do we relate it to this project?" Belle asked.

"The next step would be to see how we could recreate those conditions of good projects we remember in this project. We all know they're possible, since we've seen them."

"This is Appreciative Inquiry!" said Tara. "I was in a session on AI at a conference last year. They use it in the US Army. Focus on what's working instead of what's wrong. It's fascinating."

"Right, though I think it's the Navy," said Paul. "Lots of organizations are adopting AI methods: banks, IT companies, government departments, trucking companies, not-for-profits, even restaurants. There's a proper methodology for doing it. We just experienced a taste of it. But taking an appreciative look at things, instead of looking at problems, puts you into a creative space instead of keeping you in the land of Mr. Fix-It. It's done that for me, anyway."

"So what's with this communication project you're doing for Emma?" Nikki asked. "I would think IT guys would be the last people to put in charge of that. Don't you all have the gene for non-disclosure? That's my husband's excuse for not telling me anything."

"Very funny, Nikki, and pretty close to the mark. I had my doubts about our suitability. I still do, some days. Emma's thinking is that we in IT have a better understanding of the problem than more highly evolved life forms. The most amazing thing about it is that simply being aware of my communication habits has made a huge difference in the way I'm interacting with people. That's true for my whole group."

"So what have you learned? A couple of people from Finance were in one of your focus groups last week," Lou said. "They don't have the non-disclosure gene. They were yapping about it all afternoon. And they say your coffee is better than ours."

"Ah, I have a secret source. I'll take you there, if you like. As for what we're learning, does anyone else want to know?"

Most of the group – even Belle – nodded in agreement. "I'll give you the executive summary, so we can get out of here at 4:30. We've started asking people about the problems with communication and got the same old list: don't know what's going on with the organization, don't see the big picture, nobody listens, nobody cares, *Us vs. Them* thinking. A couple of nice conspiracy theories surfaced, too. We asked why people don't communicate better and got the same old excuses: no time for it, not enough information, too much information, not my job and too many bad meetings. I've used them all myself. So we stopped looking at what's wrong and started asking about what's going right."

"Sort of like you did with Lou and me," said Lynnette.

"Right. At the same time, we're researching outside Forthright. We're looking at best practices, talking to other companies and consultants and reading like mad. A few big principles stand out."

Paul moved to the white board and wrote: Always On. "First of all, everything communicates and everyone is a communicator. Even if you sit on a bench like a lump, your inaction and silence send out messages."

"Next, comes evidence that the quality of communication determines how engaged people are with their work, how well they do their work and things like turnover and absenteeism. But communication like *Forthright Today* and the annual report don't matter as much as informal communication, what goes on between people on the job. Organizations can't ignore the huge role conversations play. The trick is that organizations can't control them. Individuals have control. But organizations can create the conditions for conversations to happen. So that's what we're working on. Are you with me so far?"

"Isn't that what staff meetings are for?" asked Burt.

"In theory, but staff meetings aren't always good and, sometimes, they aren't even happening. And not everyone gets the same thing from a meeting. One thing that really interested me – and helped me quite a bit – is learning that we don't all communicate the same way and we don't all respond to the same sort of information. I've been running around focused on ideas and big picture stuff and wondering why people don't understand me. They often need something I'm not providing. I can make decisions in a heartbeat, based on gut feel. Burt, on the other hand, needs to see and weigh the evidence. Lou is an ideas guy. From what I know of Belle, she needs to see the action that comes out of an idea. It's not that one method's better than the other; they're just different approaches. Since I started sizing up people's styles and giving them information the way they need it, I'm getting through to people. I'm speaking their language. It's powerful."

Paul next wrote: 100%. "Another thing is we've developed some ideas around responsibility for communication. We're thinking that each of us has to be 100 per cent accountable for how our communication is understood. We also think we need to be responsible for asking what something means if we don't understand. I think that's what happened with Taylor and the programmers. He thought he was telling us there could be delays. He may have indirectly asked for help or input. Unfortunately, he didn't check to see if he was really getting through. We weren't getting the message, but nobody asked. It didn't seem important, or we didn't want to look stupid."

"Or we just stopped paying attention because he wasn't using our style," said Lou.

"Exactly. We could have asked what it meant, in our terms. But we didn't. So when Taylor announced the delay today, we all acted like it's out of the blue. But a few things conspired to get us here."

"I really was trying to make you understand," Taylor said, crossing his arms, uncomfortable at being singled out. "For about three months."

"We sure didn't get the message," said Belle.

"We all need to be responsible for both sending and receiving the message," Paul said. "Conversation is the foundation of everything we do. You can't get anything done without talking to someone. Not a product, not a project, not a paper clip, not a thing. The only reason we're in business is to do things customers will pay for and we don't know what that is without a conversation. Even transactions can be seen as conversation between organizations, computers and clients."

He took the red marker and printed: Organization = Conversation. "Here's the weird part. I'm starting to think that an organization is just a series of conversations. If Forthright is just one big conversation, then we have to make sure we're really communicating."

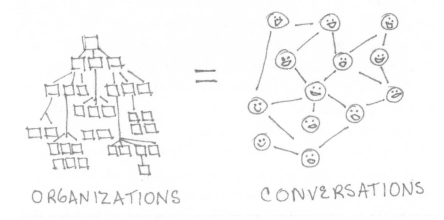

ORGANIZATIONS   CONVERSATIONS

"Organizations are conversations. We might have to think about that one," said Burt. "It's 4:25. I think this conversation is pretty much over, for today."

"I'd love to pursue this appreciative thing further," said Lynnette. "Anyone else? Maybe we could get Paul to lead a proper session."

Even Belle was interested, so Paul suggested a special session for the following week. Since Tara knew a little about the process and was good at organizing things, he asked and she agreed to help facilitate.

"This could be a big breakthrough," she said. "It could save this project."

"I don't know about saving it," Paul said, wondering what he'd just committed to, "but it will definitely change it."

As he walked through the rain to The Coffee Grounds, Paul wasn't sure he'd done the right thing in leaking some of the learning from the Talk To Me project. It wasn't organized and it was so early in the process. And to launch into it like that, with no setup, seemed quite out of order.

When he arrived at the shop, Katy was nowhere to be seen. Caryl the young barista greeted him. "Katy should be back in about five minutes. I don't think she was expecting you. Latte, skim, no cocoa, right?"

"You're good." Paul waited at the counter. He loved the energy this young woman brought to what he considered a pretty routine job. "Caryl, what do you like most about your job?"

"Well, besides an obscene discount on every amazing thing we sell, I would say it's the conversations I get into with customers. I love that. My job is really one big fascinating conversation."

At that point, Katy arrived, shaking the rain off her coat.

"Hey, Paul. What's up? I wasn't expecting you till tomorrow. Can I get you a latte?"

"Caryl's working on that. But, from you, I could use some perspective."

Paul took the usual table and watched as Katy loaded a tray with two coffees, ice water and a plate of biscuits.

"Lemon biscotti," she said as she sat down. "What's brings you here today?"

"Oh, Katy. I don't know about this gig," he said.

"The Talk To Me project?"

"And Project Delta. I tested some of my newly-minted communication ideas at the Delta meeting this afternoon and . . . actually I launched them, like grenades. I didn't think about the context, the audience, the time, place or anything. I broke every rule in my own book. Fiasco."

"If you obey all the rules, you miss all the fun. Katharine Hepburn said that. Why don't you tell me what happened."

"I don't want to remember. It was not my finest hour."

"Let's see what happened before we decide that. Start at the beginning."

"The usual cast of characters was gathered and everything was taking place according to the script we use every week. I was wondering how Burt would handle things given our meeting yesterday. Taylor, who heads up the programmers, announced a delay of seven weeks and nobody was buying his excuses. It seemed to a few of us as if he was pointing fingers at everyone else. People pointed right back at him. A big scapegoat chase."

"Sounds like fun."

"Anyway, Lynnette Benson, from Marketing, whose group is actually funding this project, made a big speech about consequences and accountability and crappy communication and – well, one thing led to another and you can guess what happened next."

"No, Paul, I can't. What happened?"

"I stepped in. I got up on my high horse, and unleashed my ideas about conversation. I'm not even sure they were really my ideas. I don't remember even thinking about some of them until I heard them come through my lips. That is so not like me."

"Don't be so sure," Katy said. "Which ideas did you unleash?"

"Taking responsibility for how you're understood. Making sure you get what you need to understand. I touched on communication styles. And I waded into the area of asking appreciative questions, which I know approximately nothing about. Now, I'm on the dime to facilitate a session next week."

"Great!" said Katy.

"Not!" said Paul. "I don't really know enough about it.

"And then I went on to say that Forthright, or any organization, is just a series of conversations – that any organization is a great big conversation. Where did that come from?"

"Organizations as conversations. What a concept. Doesn't sound familiar. I guess you made it up," Katy said. "Who cares where it came from? What does it mean for you?"

Paul paused for a two-second eternity. "If the organization is a conversation, then we've been focusing on the wrong stuff for a long time. It means that this Talk To Me thing is too important to be left to the likes of me. And if the organization is a conversation that's anything like the conversations we've had in Project Delta, we're an organization in deep trouble."

"May I make an observation?" Katy asked. Paul nodded.

"Most organizations could probably be considered dysfunctional if communication quality were the only criterion. But knowing that won't help you move ahead, though it does make your Talk To Me project look more important than ever."

"Let's get back to the meeting," Paul said, taking another biscuit.

"So, when you suggested paying attention to the team's conversations, did people throw rocks?"

"A couple of pebbles. Nothing serious."

"So, how do you think it went?"

"Well, nobody fell asleep."

"Can I make another observation?" Katy asked.

Why did she always ask for permission when he was dying to know what she thought?

"I think what you did today was great."

"Wish I did," said Paul.

"You will. Trust me. This is just the beginning."

What's Going On Here

"The single biggest problem in communicating is the illusion that it has taken place." That quotation, often attributed to George Bernard Shaw, describes the situation the Delta Project team finds itself in. Wherever there are two people or more, miscommunication is possible and, unfortunately, all too frequent.

Over the life of the project, Taylor Flynn thought he was communicating the seriousness of the challenges for his programming group and the technological difficulty involved. The others thought they were listening, yet they didn't hear any alarm bells going off. What happened? Where did communication break down?

In Chapter One, when we heard about the project, Paul described Taylor's participation this way:

Next, Taylor Flynn, who managed the burgeoning group of program-mers, would complain about the technical challenges and risks necessitated by Forthright's decision to adapt an existing system rather than custom build one. Then he went on to describe the week's progress in such detail that even Burt's eyes glazed over.

Unhappy with the buy vs. build decision, Taylor continued to discuss it often and at length. This caused the rest of the group to tune out when he was speaking. Taylor didn't realize that in repeating a monologue on a past decision that's unlikely to be changed, he was wasting time and annoying people. We can bet he was unaware he was doing it.

Taylor also provided more detail than was needed for the context of the meeting. This is another way to lose your audience's attention. We need to provide enough evidence to satisfy Guardians and Artisans without overdoing it. Someone with a personally important point to make often feels a need to provide stacks of evidence supporting the case. Unfortunately, this can backfire by confusing people. When confused, the human brain defers decisions.

This perceived need to provide heaps of evidence is made worse if the presenter uses inductive, rather than deductive, reasoning. Inductive reasoning sounds like this:

- Here's a bit of background.
- Here's some more evidence.
- Oh, and there's this.
- And while that was happening, this was going on.
- And here's some more data.
- And here's what I think we should do about it.

People who use inductive reasoning pile one idea on top of another in hope that the audience will eventually get the point. It's long, slow and painful for those on the receiving end as they try to figure out where the tale is headed. Those who use inductive reasoning often complain that people don't listen to them.

While slowly and steadily leaking clues works well in a mystery novel, it is seldom effective in persuasion. If the audience doesn't know your point, most of what you say will sound like, "Blah, blah, blah, blah, blah."

We have greater success with deductive reasoning, which sounds something like this:

- Here's what I think we should do.
- Here's one reason.

- Here's some more evidence.
- And here's some more.
- And finally, there's this.

Deductive reasoning makes the point first and, then, presents evidence showing why it's a good idea. It gives the receiver's brain a framework for paying attention.

Had Taylor made his point clearly, crisply, and used deductive reasoning, he would have gained and held people's attention and found support in time to prevent the mess he is in.

When we send a message out into the universe, we believe others will understand and act on it. We're often surprised when they don't. But sending a message is just one step. Receiving is the next. Interpreting, understanding and processing have to take place in the receiver's brain before the information can be translated into action.

Recall Katy's 100 per cent rule, introduced in Chapter Four. It suggests each of us is responsible for how a message is sent and for how it is received. It's a good model to make us aware of our need to communicate in a listener-sensitive way, using the appropriate style, channel, time and message.

Realistically, 100 per cent of the conversation is more than we can control. The listener determines how the message is understood. Nevertheless, there's much we can do to position what we say to gain and hold someone's attention, and then influence the decision about how to respond.

Understanding the different Communication Styles can help us position our messages better. If we don't know people's styles, it's good to provide a mix of logic, evidence, vision, action and impact on people.

It also helps to be aware of how we're listening. Biases, filters, preconceived ideas, and unchallenged beliefs can interfere with what we hear. Our human tendency to want to be right makes us listen for information that supports our view.

As a child, you may have played the Telephone Game, in which a message, whispered in one person's ear and passed from person to person, is distorted or turned to gibberish by the time it reaches the last person in the chain. In communication workshops, even savvy adults focused on communication will twist the phrase until the meaning is obscure or very different. We don't really hear what was said because our brains interpret the message based on our experience.

Often, we talk to each other, not with each other. A meeting becomes a series of monologues instead of a dialogue. It is only when – as the literal meaning of conversation suggests – we turn together to explore ideas that the real connection and collaboration begin.

It is in conversation that expectations and goals can be shared, and trust can be built.

It is in conversation that the work of the organization becomes real.

Do Try This At Home

In the next few conversations you participate in, what gets and keeps your attention?

Examine your listening patterns.

- Are you curious about what the other person is saying?
- Are you listening for new ideas?
- Are you listening for information that supports your views?
- Are you waiting for a chance to make your own point?

Write down three to five things you wish you had heard at the last meeting you were at.

Write down three to five things you wish you had said at the last meeting you were at.

Ask yourself why these things weren't said.

CHAPTER

9

Catching the Virus

P aul was gathering his thoughts for his weekly call with Emma when his Blackberry rang.

"Hi Paul. It's Lynnette. Got a minute?"

"Maybe five. What's up?"

"First I want to thank you for intervening at the Project Delta meeting. If you hadn't stepped in when you did, I might have wandered into Crazy Person Land. It's been known to happen."

"I don't think anyone saw a crazy person in the room. Frankly, I thought you stayed pretty cool, given the circumstances. You're the client on this project. Your division is footing the bill at nine thousand dollars a day. You might be entitled to be just a bit cranky. Besides, what you said was important and it started a conversation that could get us all moving in the same direction again."

"That's the other reason I'm calling. To give you a heads up that Ron Walters is interested in your conversation project."

"As in, helping with it? Shutting it down? What?"

"As in being a client. Emma's been singing your praises at the Management Committee. Then yesterday, at the gym or somewhere, Lou Amyot was making some noise about there finally being a breakthrough on Project Delta and it was all your doing."

"Whoa! We've hardly started. It may not be a breakthrough. Let's not count the chickens before they hatch."

"Hey, Lou's a finance guy. They count everything. He's probably got those chickens on a spreadsheet. Anyway Ron's keen to see where our group might use what you're learning. And in the meantime, we could use your help on something."

"Tell me more. I'm listening."

"We want you to help us have a conversation with Taylor Flynn and the programmers. Facilitate or whatever, using some of the things you've learned on this conversation project. The appreciative questioning session next week will be really good for the project. It's the sort of thing we should do when we start any project." Lynnette paused as if she wasn't quite sure how to phrase her next remark.

"Do I hear a *however* in your tone?" Paul asked.

"Yes. In the meantime, we have this delay. We need to have a discussion that solves the immediate issue of getting a date from the programmers. Every time there's been a delay, I've sat down with Taylor and Burt, and we've hammered something out. But the usual process isn't working. They've missed every date they've promised. It's time for a different conversation. Given your role and what you're learning about communication, having you facilitate could help us get to the heart of the issue. We really need a promise we can rely on. Would you be willing?"

"Yikes! It's not really my area of expertise, but neither is anything else I've been doing lately. Ron doesn't want to do it? I'm sure he's good at this stuff."

"Ron can't be neutral and, even if he could, he wouldn't be seen as neutral. I'm suggesting Taylor and Dennis Wilson, his chief programmer, Ron and me, with you leading the discussion and keeping it from being a bun fight."

"What about Burt?"

"Do we have to? His energy is so negative. He always makes me feel like the stupidest thing alive."

"It will be more negative if we don't include him. Every time people avoid Burt because they don't want to upset him, or deal with his prickly personality, or feel like a worm – I know that feeling – we make the problem worse. When he feels left out, he gets more controlling."

Lynnette sighed. "But how do we make progress? Burt thinks he knows everything about everything and he just imposes his will. He invokes the name of the Management Committee and expects us all to bow in obedience. He impedes progress."

Paul had an impulse to defend Burt, but let it pass. "If you feel strongly about keeping him out, we could have an exploratory conversation. No decisions, just fact finding. Would that work for you and Ron?"

"Let's give it a shot. Your conference room? Tomorrow? 1:00?"

"Good. It won't be a bun fight. I'll bring cookies. Much more powerful weapons."

"Perfect. I'll organize the others. Thanks so much. There's one thing about Ron that I need to warn you about, in case he mentions it. You have to promise not to laugh."

"Can't promise. What's the issue?"

"He wants to make excellence contagious. I don't know if it's his idea or something he read in some blog. It's his latest obsession. He thinks the marketing department can spread what he calls the *Excellence Virus* through all of Forthright."

"Another customer service campaign slogan?"

"No. It's about us being role models. He knows the value of all the traditional marketing and promotional stuff. But he's convinced that getting the message through to people is more about what you do than what you say. He also knows some people don't take our department seriously. So he wants his team to be awesome examples of excellence so that it will rub off on other people."

"Super. We've got Marketing out there spreading viruses. Already Gita Vish in HR is forming a team to develop an antidote. Can't have outbreaks of excellence around here. Gotta follow the rules."

"Paul, that's mean. Remember what you said about communication styles. Not everyone thinks like you do."

"You're right, Lynnette. We Rationals can be sarcastic when we're not at our best. Bad habit. Just warn Ron not to use the word *virus* near Gita. She'll be fretting that it's not one of the diseases mentioned in the health plan. She has a high need for order and hates surprises."

"He's more likely to use that word near you. Having meaningful conversations is definitely a symptom of excellence, so he's interested in what you're up to."

"That's good. Unlike me, he's creative. I could use his ideas."

"And he's an opinion leader," said Lynnette, "which is marketer-speak for someone who can use his network to help you."

"Thanks for the translation. I like this virus idea. It's a bit sick – pun intended – but it's a great metaphor for that old strategy of leading by example. You can't mandate it, so you want people to catch it the way they catch a cold, from the environment. And Ron's right that what you do sends a more powerful message than what you say. I'll be interested in hearing his ideas."

"Cool. By the way, how are your plans coming along for next week's appreciative questioning session?"

"Tara's got it under control. She had a workbook from that conference session she spoke about. We're just following the steps. She'll be the lead facilitator and she's thrilled about that. It's a nice change from tweaking the project plan and nagging everyone for their reports. Burt doesn't seem to give her much else to do."

"Maybe that'll change when he sees her doing this sort of work. She's capable of a lot more than he knows. We're all capable of so much more than anyone knows. If we all worked at our potential, we'd surprise ourselves. On that happy note, I'll say goodbye, and go off and try to surprise myself."

"Good luck. Keep spreading that virus."

The idea of spreading excellence like a virus intrigued Paul. What if the answer to the question of how to deliver the Talk To Me program wasn't a formal program? Maybe the trick was to create something contagious. What would do that? It would require lots of people using the habits of effective conversation – and lots of people seeing evidence that they work.

If he knew anything about enrolling people to support an idea it was that they have to understand how something would benefit them and they have to see that it's possible to do it. They want to know why and they want to know how.

When he left the office, that evening, Paul wondered how he had agreed so readily added one more task to his lengthening list of things to do. Facilitating Lynnette's meeting would not be a trivial matter. He was surprised by how much he was looking forward to it.

The next morning, he stopped in at The Coffee Grounds to pick up some beans and biscotti. It was really an excuse to check in with Katy, and both of them knew it.

"Nice to see you, this morning," Katy said. "What brings you here, besides our awesome coffee?"

ASK THE QUESTION
BEHIND THE QUESTION

"I have a chance to test some of our conversation theories this afternoon. The marketing people have asked me to facilitate a deep and honest discussion with the Project Delta developers. Any words of advice?"

"It's all about the questions. For every question you want to ask, think about the question that lies underneath it. Ask your question and ask the question behind the question."

"I'm not sure I know what you mean."

"You have to be really curious. It's rarely a problem when the conversation's about actions, ideas or things – surface stuff. But for a conversation about commitment, you need to dig deep. You have to ask questions that may be uncomfortable to answer. They may even be uncomfortable to ask. They unearth motivation and feelings. They address accountability, consequences, capacity and even competence."

"Ouch! I see what you mean by uncomfortable questions."

"There's a kind of insurance policy that you can take out, right at the start. Can you guess what I mean?"

"Lemon biscotti? Just kidding, though I will take a dozen. I'm guessing the smart thing would be to establish, early on, where their interests overlap and focus on collaboration, not differences. As in most situations, both sides want this to work. They probably have more in common than they know."

"That's part of it. The big idea is that you have to make it safe for people to recognize and speak the truth. Knowing that everyone's aiming for the same goal can help with that. So is knowing where the agendas may differ. The truth may not be the easy answer. It may seem incompatible with organizational norms, such as always being agreeable, or habitually meeting unreasonable deadlines, or heading in whatever direction the wind is blowing on the executive floor. I'll bet that one of the reasons the project is behind schedule is that your developers were pressured to say, 'Yes' when they knew they should say, 'No.' Sometimes, in business, you get the feeling that 'No' isn't an acceptable answer, even when it's the right one."

Katy was right. Paul imagined he was guilty on every count. "So we get pushed into commitments we can't possibly honor and make ourselves crazy trying to fulfill them. And we look and feel like losers when we don't."

"Exactly. So when someone wants you to do something, you have options: 'Yes,' 'No' or what else?"

"A compromise?"

"Yes – a counter offer. It could be a compromise between two courses of action, or it could be a different action altogether."

"So we always have three options, 'Yes,' 'No' and a counter offer."

"There are more," Katy said. "You can ask for more time to decide and you can ask for more information. Those are two options that often get forgotten in business situations, especially when the situation feels urgent. People make commitments without having all the facts or having enough time to study them. Then they can't keep their promises."

"I'm sure that was at work for Taylor and his group," Paul said. "With technology projects you never have enough time or facts. You always have to live with a certain amount of uncertainty and give it your best guess."

"Right," said Katy, "but if you get beaten up every time you guess wrong, what happens?"

"You get really cautious and conservative in your guessing. Then you get beaten up for that. As long as there is fear around, it's hard to get honesty. Fear and honesty are incompatible. But how do you make sure that everybody knows they're safe? No judging, no repercussions for telling it like it is – and no beatings, metaphorical or otherwise."

"You start, just as you suggested, by finding the mutual purpose. Then what might you do?"

Katy's pattern of tossing the question back to him now amused Paul instead of annoying him. He'd grown used to it and recognized that thinking the issue through and creating his own answer made the idea more meaningful to him than just taking direction.

"Well, I guess you can acknowledge that, even though you've agreed on the big What and Why there are, or might be, differences in your approaches to How. You can be honest about the type of conversation you're going to have. Recognize that it won't be easy and it may be uncomfortable. There will be emotions. People may want to defend their positions, instead of listening. There may be blaming or excuse making. So we should set and agree to some ground rules around listening, respect, recognizing everyone's needs, acknowledging feelings and knowing what you'll do if people get uncomfortable."

"Sounds good to me," Katy said. "You'll also want to agree on how you'll know when the agreement is complete, when the promise has been fulfilled."

"Exit criteria. Got it."

"I think you're set. Let me know how it goes."

As he walked to the office, Paul noticed that he wasn't as eager for the afternoon meeting as he had been earlier. This was a high stakes meeting. Beyond professional responsibility, people had a high emotional investment in the project. That worried him.

When emotion entered the room, Paul usually wanted to leave. He'd withdraw from the discussion or say something to end it. Today he'd need to find a way to keep the conversation going when emotions ran high. Why hadn't he asked Katy about this? Of course, she usually made him think for himself. What did he think? Perhaps, rather than ignoring the emotion or pretending it wasn't there, they could acknowledge it and discuss its impact on the situation and the conversation. Beyond that, he didn't know.

Later that day, he took some time to prepare questions for the meeting. He read what he'd written at the café.

- Safety!!!!! (guidelines)
- Mutual purpose
- No hidden agendas
- Speak truth
- Ask question beneath question
- Acknowledge options (Yes, No, Counter Offer, More Time, More Info)
- No beatings

Taylor and Dennis were already in the conference room when Paul arrived, a few minutes before one o'clock. Lynnette and Ron slipped in and everyone took their chairs – armchairs from the lounge that Paul had arranged in a circle.

"I hope everyone's comfortable. That's why Lynnette suggested meeting here rather than our usual room. I hope you'll stay comfortable. We may have to dig pretty deeply into the facts and feelings, challenge assumptions, and see and say what's really true for us. That sort of stuff can make people uncomfortable. If we can work through it, recognize that we're uncomfortable and still keep talking, we'll come up with some reliable ideas."

Paul noticed his palms were sweaty and he sensed that familiar hot sensation in his throat. Things might, indeed, get uncomfortable. There was a lot at stake in this conversation, and he wanted to keep it light and productive. "It sounds paradoxical to be comfortable with discomfort, but it can be done if we make it safe to be honest. With that in mind, if you agree, I'd like to propose a few ground rules and you can add any you like."

Paul wrote on a flip chart: Four walls.

"You know how they say, 'What happens in Vegas stays in Vegas?' Well, this may not look like Vegas, but what happens here stays here, except what we agree to take out, like a decision or a report or request."

The five of them agreed. Paul wrote: Agendas in the open.

"To the degree we're aware of them, let's get rid of any hidden agendas. Our aim is to get a reliable date for implementation. That's the official agenda. But each of us may have other agendas that can affect the way we'll work together. For example, I want this meeting to go well because we're trying out theories that, if they work, can make me and my team look good, change the way we communicate at Forthright, and help us all live happily ever after. You may laugh at that, but if we recognize that I have an agenda around this other project, you'll notice if I sacrifice progress for process and call me on it."

He wasn't sure how to describe his other challenge. "Another thing is that I need to find a way we can all work with Burt. I know he can be a pain, but he's far from incompetent – and he's still the project manager."

"That actually links to my hidden agenda," said Ron. "I'm trying to get more familiar with how the technical groups operate. Delta is the first of a series of big projects we're planning and I feel vulnerable. Pretend you didn't just hear an SVP confess to being vulnerable. Four Walls, eh? When I talk with tech people, I don't always understand the impact of things on the schedule. I need to have realistic expectations."

"Thanks, Ron," said Taylor. "That's an agenda we don't want you to hide. We're sometimes fuzzy about what you need, too. Communication breaks down when there are all these middlemen and barriers between front line people, like you, and back office people, like us. Most of your marketing people are just names on memos. I didn't think I had a hidden agenda, but I'll adopt yours. Building a relationship with Marketing, so we have a better idea of what's going on, is my new hidden agenda. Make that unhidden, now."

"Good stuff," said Paul. "That's an example of an agenda that, now that it's in the open, will actually contribute to the discussion, now and in future."

Dennis was the next to speak. "OK, since we've got the Four Walls rule, and I'm trying to be honest, my hidden – or maybe not-so-hidden – agenda is to protect my team. I don't want to wear people out because, in this market, any one of them could make just one phone call and have another job tomorrow, probably with better pay. We have low staff turnover for the industry, but it's still high. Burnout's an issue that's definitely influencing me."

"So we'll keep that in mind," said Lynette. "I wasn't aware of a hidden agenda, although, now that Paul has mentioned it, having a better approach to dealing with Burt would be a good thing."

The group agreed to all Paul's guidelines with one amendment. "Speak the truth" became something Dennis dubbed the "Courtroom Rule: The truth, the whole truth, and nothing but the truth."

"That should get rid of any nonsense," he said.

As the conversation unfolded, the group agreed that their personal and professional credibility would not survive another delay. The target date had to be real, not a compromise designed to make executives happy.

"We need to have a meeting like this at the executive level too," said Ron. "They've been looking at schedules and dates and everyone's pointing fingers. They're not talking about the real issues. They don't know what the real issues are. We hardly know what they are."

"Do they need to know the real issues?" Paul asked. "If so, how would they find out?"

"Our reports. They make sense to us, because we're in the middle of things. Plus it's how we've always done them," Lynnette said. "Maybe we need to give the execs more of certain kinds of info and less of other stuff – probably a lot less. And we have to put it in their context, not ours, if we want it to mean something to them. That will help them make sense of this new date, whatever it is."

Next came a process Paul called, "Check the Evidence." It was drawn from the exercise Katy had shown him for reprogramming his self-talk – the second step, inquire, investigate or interrogate.

"You look at a statement or belief," he said. "Ask if it's true. Look at the evidence. Could something else be true? What else might be true? You're open to other possibilities."

"So, for example, I might think our slow pace has to do with not having enough programmers working on the project," said Dennis. "But it might be that I have the wrong ones working on it. It could be skill, not numbers."

"Or some feature I think is critical might just be nice to have?" Lynnette asked.

"Or something I understood as an order might only have been a question," said Taylor. "I bump into that all the time. Someone asks for something. We move Heaven and Earth to get it for them and then it turns out it wasn't important. Meanwhile we're falling behind on the important stuff."

"What could you do to avoid that problem?" Paul asked.

"Clarify. Find out what people mean. I'm so used to seeing everything as an order that I've stopped challenging suggestions. I just say, 'Yes, sir. No, sir. Three bags full,' like the black sheep in the nursery rhyme. Plus, I'll confess that we take some pride in figuring out how to do something tricky. Programmers love that."

"To a point," said Dennis. "But not when it adds to the backlog."

"Is that really the reason? You don't challenge because you're used to taking orders?" Paul asked?

Taylor thought for a bit. "Maybe not. I just don't like to say 'No' to people. It makes them unhappy. It makes me look uncooperative, possibly incompetent. Yikes! How dysfunctional does that sound?"

"Then we're all dysfunctional," said Lynnette. "I think it's pretty common. I certainly do that. I want everyone to love me and think I'm great at my job and a wonderful person."

"So what would you do if you didn't care what other people thought of you?" Paul asked.

Lynnette went first. "Well, I'd be – oh crap! – I'd be more honest."

Paul kept questioning. "And if you and Taylor were more honest, is it possible that people might still find the two of you cooperative, competent, great, and loveable?"

Lynnette laughed. "Oh God! Is this one of those things it's going to take 10 years of therapy to get over?"

"Maybe we can get a group rate," said Taylor.

"I don't think therapy's the answer," Ron said. "I think we have to decide what's important. Think about people you admire and trust. Are they honest? You bet. Are they effective? Yes. Are they focused on what's important? Or are they focused on what other people think of them?"

"So, coming back to Project Delta, what's important?" Paul asked. He led them through questions that addressed purpose, capability, readiness and confidence. To Paul, it seemed that, for the first time in a long time, the right people were in the room discussing the Delta Project like intelligent grown-ups. They talked for two hours.

To make sure the programmers were working on the right things, Lynnette led the group through a review of the backlogged requirements. "We'll concentrate on the must haves and kill the rest. With some of this stuff, you wonder who asked for it. I can only assume we did."

Next they examined the technological difficulty, the most popular explanation for the delay. In looking at what was true, they realized that this notion of technical challenge was actually masking a skill problem. Taylor would see about swapping some programmers in from other projects and adding a couple of contract people.

Dennis undertook to review the development time estimates at the programmer level. "I'm going to probe a bit deeper. If someone's coded something 50 times and says it takes three days, I'll believe it. If it involves something new, I'll probe for their readiness and make sure they didn't underestimate the steepness of their learning curve or overestimate their ability."

They established that Ron, as the sponsor, would deal with the executives and manage their expectations. "I'll give them the info they need, not just what we feel like giving them. I want them to really understand what they're getting and the reasons for the delay. I think they'll find – as we probably will – that the time will seem shorter in retrospect than it did in anticipation."

After the discussion, they knew the delay really would be six weeks. "You know," said Taylor, "Someone could claim that nothing's changed and we went through today's dialogue for nothing. But, you know, when I picked that date, earlier this week, I was just taking a stab in the dark. Nobody had confidence in that date – not even me. Today, I know this date is a promise we all can count on. I'm confident taking it to Burt. Anyone want to come along?"

What's Going On Here

When they began the meeting, Paul and the others knew two things. There was going to be a delay in the delivery date and they had just one more chance to get it right. Their credibility was dwindling with every delay. They were losing the organization's trust and they had stopped trusting each other. Difficulties had diminished their confidence in themselves and each other.

By acknowledging that the conversation might get uncomfortable and preparing for that, Paul offered a measure of safety for the participants. They anticipated their emotions and brought alternate personal agendas into the open. They were encouraged to share not just what they knew but also what they felt. They set ground rules to help manage the discussion, rather than just letting it wander.

By remaining curious, rather than directive or accusative, Paul avoided provoking defensiveness. People could relax and relaxation enables creativity.

Whether trust builds collaboration or collaboration builds trust was unimportant for this group. They needed both and they needed them in a hurry. Adding Paul's light-handed facilitation to their shared objectives and personal motivation accelerated the trust building process.

Trust in organizations is seen in the exchange of promises and there is a direct relationship between organizational trust and fulfilled promises.

How reliably we can agree to a commitment depends on the candor of our conversations. Whether we're asking for a commitment or giving it, conditions have to be met for it to work. We need to agree on the work to be done, the time it will be completed and the conditions of acceptance.

Accepting or making promises, without confidence that they are clearly defined and actually achievable, erodes trust. If you're a trusting person, you may accept people's promises without question. And you may be disappointed when you receive something different from what you expected. If you're not a trusting person, you'll cross-examine the promise maker on every aspect of the task, which can be hard on your relationships. Or you may build extra contingency into your planning. You only need to be disappointed once or twice before you start advancing the deadline to compensate for your promise makers' unreliability. And you only have to do that once or twice before they're on to you. Mistrust breeds mistrust.

And trust breeds trust. Setting up a safe environment for honest, open conversation is a step towards building trust. Gentle questioning about the details allows both the requester and the promise maker to examine the requirements of the task and to assess the resources, capacity and capability available to meet them.

Trust takes time to build, but you can accelerate the process by making the first move. You can start a conversation that gets you talking about the conditions for reliable commitments.

While we're thinking about trust, if the goal of the meeting was to make a decision about the date or the process to reach it, meeting without Burt Shepler was risky. Dates and processes are the project manager's business. Fortunately, Paul agreed to proceed only if the meeting was about exploring the situation and discovering information. One of the keys to an effective conversation is to know the desired outcome and have the right people taking part. Burt's input would be more useful once the rest of the team had a chance to examine what they needed – and what they needed to discuss with Burt.

Do Try This At Home

Identify a conversation you've been avoiding rather than tackling.

1. What's the best thing that will happen if you have this conversation?
2. What's the worst thing that will happen?
3. Is that likely?
4. What will happen if you don't have the conversation?
5. How can you create safety for yourself and the other participant(s)?
6. Have you ever accepted someone's commitment without knowing what they have to do to honor it?
7. Why did you do that?
8. If you were disappointed, what do you think you should have asked to ensure it could be done?
9. Have you ever made a commitment without fully understanding what it would take to honor it?
10. Why do you think the person accepted your commitment?
11. If you failed to live up to the commitment, what do you think were the consequences?
12. How do you feel when people ask you probing questions about how you will meet your commitment?
13. If you feel annoyed by these questions, how do you think they could be asked so they wouldn't be annoying?

Reporting In

A beep told Paul he had a text message. That would be Tim Lee. They could both be in the same room and Tim would still prefer to send a text rather than talk. How to get the Game Boy generation to be part of the organizational conversation had been one of the research tasks Paul had assigned to Tim. He read the message: Tlk 2 u?

Paul hated text messaging. He had neither the fingers nor the patience for it. But three months earlier, when they had started working on the Talk To Me project, he'd decided that if he wanted Tim and his crowd to move into his world of face-to-face conversation, once in a while he could join them in theirs. He typed: OK. Seconds later, Tim appeared.

"I can't believe we're sending a written report about conversation," Tim said to Paul, "but I don't really see an alternative. I thought we'd come up with something more edgy and cool. Multimedia. Performance. Pecha Kucha."

"I doubt the execs know what Betcha Hucha is. I don't," Paul replied. "Think of our written report as speaking to the executives in their language. They're used to written reports. It's how they understand things. I hear some of them still get their assistants to print out their email. This audience will focus on the content, not the box. Remember, we'll be in a conversation when we present it."

"I didn't find anything I wanted to change. I think it hangs together OK." Tim had been the last one in Paul's group to proofread the Talk To Me strategy document they were preparing for Emma and her executive team. "You know, when I first heard about this project I thought, 'I'm so outta here.' It's not exactly the kind of work I signed up for when I finished B-school and came to Forthright."

"Me neither. It's probably the weirdest project either of us will ever work on."

"I hope not," said Tim. "It was interesting. At first, I thought it was totally insane. Like, why would we be concerned with old-fashioned face-to-face stuff when we have technology to communicate with anyone, any-where, 24/7? Once we got into it, it was nothing like boring. Plus I'm a better communicator after digging into all this stuff."

"I've noticed," Paul said. "Me too. At least, that's what my wife says. I guess we learned something. I'll take one last look at the report and then we'll hit *Send* and let the fun begin. I really appreciate your help."

What a change since the day he'd first presented the conversation project to his own group. By his calculations, "outta here" was something they'd all wanted at that moment. What a distance they'd come in three months.

The document made a solid case for action, a request that might surprise the Management Committee. These people were used to being asked for funding. Over the years, Paul had been involved in projects that required millions and he'd received it. How the executives would respond to a request for personal action was anyone's guess.

He read the document for what felt like the 80th time; finding nothing more to change, Paul printed copies for the next day's meeting. He made a copy for Katy, too. She'd been on his team since the start. Well indirectly at least. He'd take her copy to The Coffee Grounds, since he wanted to bid her *Bon Voyage*. Now that Caryl had enough experience to run the shop, Katy was off to Central America for nine weeks. She'd be visiting coffee plantations with her Fair Trade group and building houses in Guatemala after that.

"All set for another adventure?" he asked when he arrived at the shop.

"Absolutely! What about you? You're presenting tomorrow, right? Sorry I won't be around to hear all about it."

"I'll share the gruesome details when you get back. And you can tell me about your travels, which will be much more interesting. In the mean time, here's a copy of the plan, so you can see what we've done with your ideas."

"Correction." Katy said. "They're your ideas. I just teased them out of you in our conversations."

"Whatever it was, I appreciate it. Your fingerprints are all over this document."

"Then let's hope it doesn't show up at a crime scene."

"It'll be a crime if the execs don't go for this plan." Paul handed the report to Katy. "I won't keep you. Have a great trip."

"Will do. Have fun tomorrow. We'll catch up in a couple of months."

By the time Katy got back, there would indeed be a lot to talk about. Paul knew his biggest challenge would be managing expectations. His employees had become conversation evangelists and held high hopes that the rest of the organization would be converted quickly. They'd seen the light. Wouldn't everyone? Was it not completely obvious that attention and applied common sense would improve just about every aspect of the way people worked together at Forthright?

"The obvious can be pretty hard for people to see," Paul had told them. "Especially if they're looking for something else. What we're proposing may be hard for some people to get their heads around. We're asking them to make changes in their personal operating systems."

The other group Paul was concerned about was the Management Committee. He knew they'd be able to grasp the concepts. The idea of doing something about the quality of face-to-face communication had been hatched in one of their meetings. In her updates, Emma had warned them that they – and she – would have to ante up some personal commitment. No, his concern was that they might be looking for results too soon. Culture change takes place in small, almost imperceptible steps. If they didn't see results quickly, would they cut everything loose?

Paul was relieved when, the next day, two committee members

volunteered that the sort of lasting change they were hoping for could take four or five years. They also seemed to accept their own responsibility to make communication a priority and they made all the right noises about being role models. Paul didn't doubt the sincerity of their intentions, though he'd wait to see them in action before declaring success.

"I think that went pretty well," Emma said, when the others had left. "Using concrete examples and success stories was a good idea. Nice break from the usual parade of pie charts showing the results of research studies. I'm always suspicious of studies. It seems as if every week there's a new study by Research Company B that says something different from what we heard on the same topic last week from Research Company A. I never know what to believe. I'd rather hear about real people."

"Yeah, I tried to provide a little something that would appeal to each of the communication styles. They seemed to get the picture. I was glad John Martini picked up on that issue of people being afraid to be honest. People who get to the executive level don't like to think there might be repercussions for saying something that might not be popular with the boss."

"The chance of someone being fired for speaking up around here is pretty slim," said Emma. "It's not justifiable, it's against policy, and it's just plain stupid. But that doesn't mean people aren't afraid it could happen to them. Even though they're wrong, the feeling is real."

Emma paused. "I have to thank you for including that suggestion that we executives stop saying, 'Don't bring me problems; bring me solutions.' I hadn't realized it could be risky."

"I've used that phrase myself. It's in the How To Be A Manager lexicon. But when we say we don't want to hear about problems, people who don't have a solution figured out won't come to us. We'll never know what the problems are. That's one reason we need to address the fear of speaking up."

Emma thought for a moment. "I think if we can get people talking, especially talking from a positive stance, the fear will dissipate. But for some people, the fear inhibits talking, so it's hard to use talking as the remedy. That's why it's going to be important for bosses – you and all of us – to lead by example. We need to start the conversation and invite others in. Someone has to go first."

"Guess that's us."

"This reminds me of some work I did when I was at the bank," Emma said. "When I joined to work on the turnaround strategy, the prevailing attitude was, 'When this organization gets its act together, I'll get mine together.' It was obvious to one and all. And it was deeply de-motivating. That attitude showed up in customer service, employee morale, productivity, our corporate reputation, and the bottom line. An interview comment from a long-serving senior manager was: 'We've lost our pride.' That still gives me goose bumps."

"And did you get it back?"

"In our work to turn the company around, we looked for, and found individuals, from the CEO to the front lines, who weren't going to wait for the organization to get its act together. They were the organization. They would get their act together. They would do what was possible and be who they were capable of becoming. They ignored the cynics and skeptics. They found others who joined in. They caught possibility thinking and your Talk To Me attitude the way they might have caught a cold."

"Hmmm. Did Ron Walters get his idea of the Excellence Virus from you?" Paul asked.

"No, but I like the idea. I'll have to ask him about it." Emma typed a reminder in her Blackberry.

"OK, so back to the bank. Other things were going on to create an environment that signaled change was possible. Operational improvements took place, HR policies were revamped, and employee publications started sending out messages about real people and real changes and what the organization really stood for. We shone a spotlight on individuals, departments or project teams who demonstrated they were paying attention to what was important for reaching our big goals for service, engagement, productivity, reputation, and profit."

Paul noticed Emma had switched on her CEO-at-the-podium delivery style.

She continued. "The real change, however, was taking place when individuals, one at a time, took a chance and went first. These people said, 'Let's see what might be possible,' instead of, 'Let's wait and see.' With time, others came on board. Most people in organizations want to be helpful and do a good job. They want to be happy and feel pride in their work. They want to believe in a better future. A lot of them just need someone else to go first." Emma came to a stop and finally took a breath.

"Sorry for the monologue. I was really excited by that work and once I get started, I can go on for days. My point is that I think that's how it's going to happen here at Forthright. We'll find the people willing to go first."

"Right you are, Emma. Now, if you'll excuse me. I'd better go and talk to some of them. My team's going to want to know how our meeting went."

"I'll get over and do it in person later today, but could you give them my thanks? I knew you guys would do great work."

What's Going On Here

Building a conversation culture starts with individuals before it can move to groups or organizations. Someone has to go first. People willing to make the first move make it easier for others to break out of old habits and tired ways of thinking. Change happens one person at a time, one conversation at a time, one conscious moment at a time. It can and, maybe, has to start with you.

The minute you notice you want to be a more effective communicator, your perceptions and behavior start to change. Simple awareness can ignite a spark of desire for things to be different. You want to close the gap between what is and what could be, between who you are and who you want to be. You start to notice the habits that grew out of our society's inattention to conversation, and you work to break them. Awareness is always the start of the process.

Be warned. That spark of desire may cause discomfort. First, there's that deeply ingrained human fear of the unknown that causes our preservation instincts to battle our urge to change. The amygdala,[10] that part of our brain that drives the "fight, flee or freeze" mechanism, saved our skins when we had to be ready for encounters with a saber-toothed tiger. Today, the tigers are gone, but the amygdala still detects deviations from our usual patterns and its voice says, "Don't go there!" That need for safety fights the impulse to try something new.

The second reason is that we've learned to be wary. Our ancient need for safety also drives a desire to conform. When humans were hunters and gatherers, not being a member of the group meant you might not get dinner. Or it could mean you'd be dinner for that saber-tooth tiger.

SOMEONE HAS TO TAKE THE FIRST STEP

Learning to be comfortable with discomfort is a key to the Talk To Me attitude. Doing something that is really important, such as creating better work and a better workplace, will often take you to the edge of your comfort zone. Perhaps paradoxically, with the first step outside its perimeter, your comfort zone expands.

As you develop the habits and attitude that bring you into real, meaningful conversations, you will influence the others around you. You'll say things like, "Please help me understand your thinking on that," rather than, "I don't agree," and, "What can we do now?" rather than. "How did we get into this mess?" In each pair, the first question invites connection and trust. The second invites defensiveness and fear.

When you first adopt the Talk To Me approach, it may feel like a lonely pursuit. Managing expectations, especially your own, will be critical to success. Cultural change doesn't happen quickly. It's not something you can fix with a pill, potion or program. It takes more time than we would wish to develop new norms and standards of what is desirable and acceptable behavior. There will be no thunderbolts or choirs of angels to tell you that you're on the right path. This is evolution, not revolution. It's incremental, almost imperceptible, until you notice, one day, that you go to meetings that make progress, you seem to know what's going on and you feel more energy around you at work.

If there is a secret to this, it's that it begins with you, as an individual, and it grows with you, working with a group of like-minded people. Anthropologist Margaret Mead said: "Never underestimate the power of a small group of committed people to change the world. In fact, it is the only thing that ever has." Find these people in your organization and in your life. Enroll them in the challenge of creating meaningful conversations. Together you will reap the rewards.

Do Try This At Home

1. What one action can you take, today, to engage in a real conversation?

2. List some phrases you can add to this conversation that will create connection and trust.

3. List some phrases you can eliminate to reduce defensiveness and fear.

4. Who and where are the people who are likely to join with you in developing a Talk To Me culture in your organization?

5. How can you begin a conversation with them that will lead to better communication in your workplace?

In Retrospect

"**N**ice to see you!" Katy called out from behind the counter as Paul entered The Coffee Grounds.

"Welcome back. How was your trip?"

"Fantastic, but more on that later. How's the project going?"

"How much time do you have?"

"Caryl managed without me for two months. I think she might give me a half hour or so. Caryl?"

"Works for me," said the barista. "I'll bring the coffees."

"So?" Katy said, taking the usual table. "What happened?"

"I would love to say that we sent out a memo, everyone jumped on board, Forthright Financial changed, overnight, and we all lived happily ever after."

"And I would love to believe you, except that I know better. This stuff doesn't happen in a few months."

"Still, a lot has happened. The Management Committee – Emma and her execs – jumped on board from the start. I shouldn't have been surprised, since the original idea for a project like this came out of one of their meetings. I don't get the sense they're just tagging along because Emma's keen on it."

"That would annoy her," Katy said.

"We started with an appreciative questioning session. The execs had heard about the ones we did for the Project Delta team, Finance Group, and the Marketing Department and they were very keen to go through it themselves."

"Did you run the session?"

"Tara and I did. She's got a real gift for this sort of work, probably because she's so interested in it. She got some formal training in Appreciative Inquiry, and she's training a network of facilitators across the organization. At the next annual Managers' Meeting, the first day will be devoted to AI. It'll be a real change from the corporate pep rally with the expensive keynote speaker. We're going to have people talk to each other."

"That will set an excellent tone. Was that Emma's idea?"

"No, and you will never guess whose idea it was."

"Tara's?"

"Close. Her boss. Burt Shepler."

"The man formerly known as The Project Manager From Hell?"

"The very one! Strangely enough, he really latched on to AI. It looks enough like a methodology to meet his need for order and control, and there's heaps of data on it from reliable organizations, like the Army."

"The Navy."

"Whatever. By now, the Army must be doing it, too."

"So you're doing appreciative inquiry on both a large and small scale. Cool. What else?"

"Gita Vish and her mob in HR have actually turned out to be helpful. I don't know why they have such a bad reputation. Maybe it just comes with the turf. Anyway interpersonal communication is already on every job description. For senior people, it's been there for years. But people just ignored it."

"And now?"

"It's going to be on the performance reviews. They're working on comprehensive behavioral descriptions of good interpersonal communication for every level in the organization. That's going in the new competency model, which was being revised anyway. I think that's why Gita was willing to make the change."

"How convenient. How do you feel about that?"

"Excited. Curious. Hopeful. I needed to find a way to get people to take the conversation principles seriously. The idea's based on that old adage, 'What gets measured gets done.' So this will get measured. Some people have the impression that it's risky to speak up. They're fearful. It seemed that the organization needed to grant permission to engage in honest, productive, two-way conversation. Then, they needed to show people what that looks like. What signals permission more strongly than asking people to do something and following up?"

"When does all this take effect?"

"Not till next year. You can't start measuring people on something they didn't know about. But HR is already communicating about the new competencies. And the Training Department has built or bought all sorts of learning tools to use along with some in-person training sessions and webinars. Our group wasn't keen on formal training, since we thought the Talk To Me attitude could spread like a virus. Gita convinced us that a training program gives people a common vocabulary for the principles, gives them a safe environment to try out behaviors, and makes sure all the key points are covered. So we're giving the idea a chance."

"Are you comfortable with it?"

"Lisa and Tim from my team worked with the developers. Now that I've seen some prototypes, I'm comfortable. There's a pilot of the live training running tomorrow. What I've seen looks great."

"No rope climbing or costumes?"

"Not a Swiss watch or feather boa in the plan. There are a lot of exercises, so people get to practice using the language of possibility, accountability and co-operation. There'll be some pretty robust follow-up tools and templates online, and some worksheets for planning conversations, especially, tricky conversations, like performance reviews and discussions about punctuality."

Katy grinned. "I can see you're excited about this."

"There's more. The next phase will involve conducting effective meetings, which should make a huge difference. And we're looking for a way to build managers' coaching skills. You might want to advise on that one."

"You know where to find me. How will you know if the program's working?"

"We're building some questions on face-to-face communication into the Employee Opinion Survey. That's obvious and measurable in terms of positive responses. It happens every year, so we can track progress. We should see whether there's behavioral change in the performance reviews, since employees and bosses are going to have to discuss behavior. We can track how often people use the online planning tools. And while we won't be able to isolate the effect of better conversations, we should see it in fewer employee complaints, lower turnover rates, and more accurate time estimates on projects. There's also got to be a way to pin a dollar value on time saved by getting things right the first time by making sure everyone understands. It would have to rely on people's time estimates."

"What could get in the way of success?"

"Hey, I thought you were Ms. Keep It Positive!"

"We have to know where the traps are so we can avoid them."

"I see two hurdles. Both involve incorrect beliefs first is the old one I came up with for myself on Day One. 'I'm not a good communicator. I'm no good at this touchy-feely stuff.' The other is a belief that conversation takes too much time. Some people may need to see evidence that a conversation that explores issues and ends in understanding takes way less time than the screw-ups that result from issuing orders in meetings, memos and emails. Joe Granberg's corporate communications people are going to help by publicizing case studies and success stories as we find them."

TALK TO ME
PRICE TAG

o Time
o INVOLVEMENT
o COURAGE
o SKILL
o WILL

"You realize that some people won't change," Katy said.

"Yeah, we know. But if we can suggest that not sharing information, not showing respect for others' ideas, and not clarifying for understanding as antisocial behavior, maybe they'll get the idea."

"So how do you feel? Can you take a moment to reflect on what Talk To Me has done for you?"

"Hmmm. I'm not the same uptight, resistant guy who walked into The Coffee Grounds all those months ago and let you talk him into taking on the project."

"You wanted it."

"You're right. I just didn't want to admit it to anyone, especially not to myself. It was so out of my domain."

"It was out of your comfort zone. And what happened when you stepped out of your comfort zone?"

"For one thing, the comfort zone got bigger. I changed my expectations about what I'm good at and what I'm capable of. I had this picture of what I was, what I was supposed to be, what I was pretending to be at work. All this looking at how I communicate and how I see possibility showed me just how restricted my view of myself was. Now I'm thinking bigger."

"May I make an observation?"

"Yeah?"

"You mention what you were, what you were supposed to be, what you were pretending to be. You didn't mention what you wanted to be. Or who you wanted to be. Is there anything to that?"

Paul paused. "What I wanted to be – besides good at my job and well compensated for it – was never on my radar. It is now. Who do I want to be at work? I want to be myself. What do I want to be? I want to be understood. It's not that complicated."

At that moment, Emma drifted into the café.

"Welcome back, Katy. And look who else is here. Did I miss hearing about your trip?"

"No, we've been talking about real conversations, and how you're going to arrange for more of them at Forthright."

"My favorite topic," Emma said. "There's been a lot of progress since that day I called and asked you to take on this project."

Emma turned to Paul. "Did Katy ask you the question yet?"

"What question?"

"The one that shook up my career. What one thing, if you could make it happen, would make you love your work?"

"I remember that," Katy said. "Did you tell Paul your answer?"

"No," Paul said, "she was saving that story for another day. This might be considered another day. Emma?"

"I'm here to listen to Katy's story, not to tell you mine, but I'll keep it brief. You may have noticed that I do love my work, at least, most of the time. So I made it happen – or something did. The thing that makes me love my work is that I can be myself, plain, honest, unvarnished Emma. That lets me deal with what's important and be my best and do my best. I think that's what everyone wants."

"No kidding," Paul and Katy said in unison.

"Now, before you tell us about your adventures in Guatemala, I have a question for Paul," Emma said.

"Is there a chance you can swing by my office tomorrow afternoon? Maybe around 4:00 or 4:30. I've got an interesting opportunity, and I'm hoping you'll agree to work with me on it."

What's Going On Here

Paul Hunchak's story has a happy ending. Yours can too.

The Talk To Me mindset is something anyone can develop and use to invite connection and collaboration. It's something you can start immediately and without large infusions of cash. However, other forms of investment are necessary, including time, involvement, courage, skill, and will.

Time: Like most good things, this approach to communication isn't something you can achieve overnight or without some attention. Still, adopting the practices and tools in this book takes far less time and effort than repairing the damage done by serial miscommunication. The energy you invest is a bargain price for driving ambiguity, unnecessary conflict, confusion and discouraging words out of your workplace.

Involvement: Building a conversation culture involves people in every level of an organization. One person can make a difference, but the change comes sooner as more people are involved. It's not something that can be left to executives or assigned to managers, although, as leaders, these people are key players. Encouraging everyone to learn and practice Talk To Me principles as part of doing business will shorten the time required and extend the benefits.

Courage: Sometimes the other people in the conversation aren't going to like the content of your communication. Perhaps the news is bad; for example, they aren't getting the promotion, they haven't performed up to standards, their attendance or punctuality must improve, or you cannot fund their request. Maybe the idea is bad; for example, you have serious reservations about a proposed action. As always, speaking directly and honestly is essential. It sometimes takes courage to resist the temptation to sugar coat the message or to avoid the discussion altogether. It's easier to find that courage when you know how to use language that invites response rather than incites reaction.

Skill: Such language can be learned informally. We've all observed the way individuals who interact adopt each other's buzzwords or phrases. Think of the speed with which "drill down," "bleeding edge," "thought leader," and "take it offline" have spread through the business world. People pick up the language they hear around them. When you model language that invites understanding and collaboration, others pick it up. To speed up the process, you can shine a spotlight on positive language and conversation habits in formal learning sessions.

Will: Perhaps the most important investment is the willingness to use the principles and the language of real conversation. Make it part of your operating system. And be the one willing to do it first. The Talk To Me attitude requires action and commitment. Think of the advice Yoda, that famous Jedi knight and part-time management guru, gave young Luke

Skywalker when he was trying to lift the spacecraft out of the swampy space goop, in *Star Wars*: "Do or Do Not. There is no Try."

So, if an effective communicator you would be, then do and do not these things, you must. Feel the power, you will. Enjoy the results, you will. Trust in the process, you must.

DO	DO NOT
Be aware in conversations	Operate on autopilot
Ask questions	Give orders
Need to be curious	Need to be right
Use words that invite responses– how	Use words that shut down dialogue – who, why
Probe for commitment and capacity when making or accepting commitments	Accept and make commitments without question
Focus on the conversation	Multitask
Look for possibility	Look for problems
Use language of possibility – what if, imagine, how might	Use language of problems – what's wrong, why did/didn't
Use language of accountability – I will, will you	Use vague language – try, better, improve
Use language that invites collaboration – Let's, can we, let's find a way to	Use language that promotes resistance – you need, you must, that's just how it is
Ask for what you want	Be indirect, hope they read minds
Say what needs to be said (be sure it needs to be said)	Say what they want to hear
Clarify if you don't understand	Pretend you understand
Be sure others understand – ask	Assume others understand
Acknowledge emotions, yours and others'	Ignore emotions
Recognize diverse styles	Act as if one message fits all
Talk to the right people	Involve the uninvolved
Nurture but challenge people	Nurture without challenge; Challenge without nurture
Know it is possible	Think it cannot be done
Listen to what people say and respond as appropriate	Assume you know what someone will say before s/he speaks
Build supportive environments	Tolerate poor performance

People in organizations around the world have learned the ways of conversation and created communication cultures in their workplaces. You don't need to meet with Yoda in the Degoba System or with Katy De Marco at The Coffee Grounds to find your way, although coaching can get you there faster.

What you need to remember is that an organization is a series of conversations. There's an old saying which states an organization is only as good as its people. We might amend that to suggest an organization is only as good as the conversations of its people, as it is only through conversation that work happens.

Do Try This At Home

You won't be surprised to discover that your final fieldwork is to put the tools in this book into practice. You may want to start with a review of the exercises in the previous chapters – or do them, if you haven't already. Then consciously start incorporating these techniques into your conversational style. You may be surprised how quickly they become part of your natural repertoire.

Catch yourself when you use phrases that encourage defensiveness or fear and replace them with positive language. There's no shame in saying, "That didn't sound good. What I meant to say was this."

There are useful ideas in the appendices.

- *Appendix One* is the executive summary of Paul's Report to Emma and the Mananagement Committee. Some of the recommendations may be useful in your organization.
- *Appendix Two* is the Talk To Me "Minifesto." It describes the reasons behind this book and the opportunity that's created when we communicate consciously.
- *Appendix Three* is Katy's Booklet, *Communication Styles: A Field Guide*. Along with the assessment to determine your own style, you'll find descriptions of the four communication styles so you

can learn how to spot them and talk to them. Having insight into people's styles will help you present information the way they like it. It will also give you some clues about what to expect in their communication.

- *Appendix Four* links you to web sites, articles, and books that can provide more detail about the tools and ideas explored here. As new information and tools are developed to support the concepts in this book, they'll be available at www.talktomebook.com

- *Appendix Five* is Katy's recipe for Chocolate Chaos Biscotti. I just had to include it because they are so good.

Finally – and most importantly – deep and powerful learning comes from simply getting out and doing something. Being in conversation with others, fully conscious, deeply curious, and truly present, will build your skills. Do this and you'll see an invitation to Talk To Me as a pleasurable adventure.

———••——

Endnotes

Chapter 1

1. Meaning of "conversation." http://www.etymonline.com/index. php?term=conversationv March 31, 2012

Chapter 3

2. Jay Cross, *Informal Learning: Rediscovering the Natural Pathways that Inspire Learning and Performance.* (San Francisco, Pfeiffer, 2007), 17.

3. Microsoft News Centre. *Survey Finds Workers Average Only Three Productive Days per Week.* http://www.microsoft.com/presspass/ press/2005/mar05/03-15threeproductivedayspr.mspxv March 31, 2012

Chapter 4

4. David Rock, SCARF: A Brain-based Model for Collaborating with and Influencing Others (first published in the Neuroleadership Journal). http://www.your-brain-at-work.com/files/NLJ_SCARFUS.pdf March 31, 2012

5. Marcus Buckingham and Curt Coffman. *First, Break All The Rules.* (New York, Simon & Shuster, 1999). 36

6. Monte Enbysk. Bad Communicator, Bad Boss (Generally) http:// www2.owen.vanderbilt.edu/david.owens/Press/Monte%20 Enbysk%20-%20Bad%20communicator,%20bad%20boss%20 %28generally%29%20-%20Microsoft%20bCentral.htm March 31, 2012

7. Robert Holland http://robertjholland.wordpress.com/2011/04/05/5-things-employees-want-from-communication/ March 31,2012

8. Martin Shovel. http://www.trainingzone.co.uk/item/184720 March 31, 2012

9. David Rock *op cit*

Chapter 10

10. Daniel Goleman. *Primal Leadership.* (Boston, Harvard, 2002). 28-29

Paul's Report – Executive Summary

FORTHRIGHT FINANCIAL SERVICES

Talk To Me Project – Executive Summary

Conversation is the most powerful business tool available today.

Forthright Financial has an opportunity to improve both quality and productivity through attention to interpersonal communication. The Talk To Me project, a three-month study conducted within the Operations Group, invited more than 50 employees and contractors associated with a large project team to become conscious of the way they approach communication with their colleagues. They were given training and tools to support them in this.

The desired changes included:

- Develop and practice new methods for managing meetings, with the focus on outcomes and decisions
- Handle reporting activities in customizable online reports, redesigned for relevance and readability
- Conduct regular assessments (via survey) of communication effectiveness, to maintain awareness

- Build closer ties between the sponsor/users and the project development team
- Design and promote support tools such as checklists, toolkits, and eLearning
- Recognize participants' differing information needs and styles of communication

Individual actions included:

- Assess one's own communication style, using online assessment and discussion
- Assume responsibility for understanding, both as sender and receiver of information and knowledge
- Focus on identifying shared context and goals, rather than points of difference
- Speak up respectfully, yet courageously, about important issues

A project retrospective, supported by an anonymous participant feedback survey, showed that:

- Project team members had a clearer understanding of the project's objectives and were more committed to it than they had been before the Talk To Me project began.
- They better understood their roles and how they intersected with and supported the roles of others.
- People experienced greater collaboration, less frustration and sensed improved morale on the team.

To establish an organization-wide benchmark, formal measurement of these dimensions will be included in the annual Employee Opinion Survey, which takes place in May.

Recommendations:

- Build responsibility for communication into the performance descriptions of all Forthright employees and contractors and evaluate their performance against desired communication competencies, to be included in the new Forthright Competency Model, already under revision.

- Develop or source learning programs that develop conversation skills: consensus building, finding common context, recognizing communication styles and preferences, disagreeing without being disagreeable, appreciative inquiry, emotional and social intelligence, etc.

- Use the executive team as role models in encouraging and supporting effective conversation practices after ensuring they are trained and supported, themselves.

- Involve all functional areas of Forthright in seeking and spotlighting success stories and share these via both formal and informal communication channels.

Financial outlay will be primarily for the learning programs and will be determined in conjunction with Human Resources Department.

The primary resource required is commitment on the part of the executive team to serve as role models for effective interpersonal communication.

APPENDIX

Talk To Me Minifesto

Nobody sets out to communicate badly. Still, it happens. And the world cannot afford it. Underlying almost every troubled situation is a gap between what is intended and what is understood and acted on. Closing that gap involves:

- Clarity,
- Context,
- Connection,
- Collaboration, and
- Courage.

To truly communicate with others, we must first understand:

- Who we are,
- Who they are, and
- What both need – from each other and from the world.

Authentic communication sparks the spirit that enables humans together to be profoundly more effective than humans alone.

Principles:

- Real conversation is the most powerful business tool anyone will ever use.
- Communication is a learned and learnable skill.
- To be truly understood is the goal – and the gift – of human communication.
- Most conversation occurs without careful, conscious thought. To really communicate, we must be conscious of what we are doing.
- We don't know what we've really said until we see what the audience does in response.
- The words we say and write are the words we hear and see – and those stimuli shape our experience of the world.
- These words also shape others' experience. Our words create our world.
- The first and most important conversation is the one we have with ourselves; it's the source of all others.

Katy's Booklet

Communication Styles
A Field Guide

by Katy De Marco

"If a man does not keep pace with his companions, perhaps it is because he hears a different drummer. Let him step to the music which he hears, however measured or far away."
–Henry David Thoreau

It doesn't take a genius to notice that people don't all operate the same way. As Thoreau suggests, we each hear and move to our own beat. Our individual ways of processing information, interacting with the world, and making decisions lead to different ways of communicating. What may seem completely logical to me may sound like utter gibberish to you. And your idea of a heartfelt message may seem like delusional ranting to someone else.

The goal of this booklet is to help you learn to recognize the differences in the way people communicate and understand information so you can better understand them. It also helps you adjust your own communication so you can be better understood.

Four basic patterns

When you observe people closely, you will find that most of the time you and they will use one of four fundamental patterns. We call these communication styles. For most people, all styles are present to some degree; however, we usually have one style that we use most of the time, our dominant style.

Plato, the ancient Greek philosopher, was one of the first to spot and write about four temperaments, or types, of people. He called them Artisan, Guardian, Rational, and Idealist. In the intervening centuries, scientists, philosophers, psychologists, and authors, including Aristotle, Galen, Jung, and Fromm have described human temperament and type in fours. Behavioral assessments such as the Myers-Briggs Type Indicator (MBTI) and the Keirsey Temperament Sorter have evolved from exploration of these four personality dimensions.

| Artisan | Guardian | Idealist | Rational |

We've used Plato's words to label the communication styles. If they were good enough for the most famous of all the philosophers, they're good enough for us.

Estimates suggest that, in western countries, Guardians and Artisans make up at least 80 per cent of the population. Don't be fooled by the labels. The relative scarcity of Rationals and Idealists doesn't mean that most of the population is neither rational nor idealistic,

What's YOUR Communication Style?

This simple quiz can help you determine your typical style. There are no right or wrong answers – the correct answer is the one that is most like you. Sometimes the choice is easy as you have a clear preference. If two or more things seem true for you, choose the one that's true more often.

Circle the answer that is most true for you.

1. I would rather be known for:
   - a. Doing things properly
   - b. Doing things cleverly
   - c. Doing things from the heart
   - d. Doing things creatively

2. I feel good about myself when I use:
   - a. My dependability
   - b. My intellect
   - c. My people skills
   - d. My ingenuity

3. I tend to trust:
   - a. Tried and true methods
   - b. Reason and logic
   - c. My intuition
   - d. My instincts

4. I'd like to have more:
   - a. Safety and security
   - b. Efficient ways of doing things
   - c. Self-awareness
   - d. Adventure

5. I like to work with:
   - a. Processes
   - b. Ideas
   - c. People
   - d. Tools

6. My advice is:

        a. Be careful
        b. Be smart
        c. Be friendly
        d. Be flexible

7. I'd rather have:

        a. Stability
        b. Knowledge
        c. Wisdom
        d. Spontaneity

8. My top strength is:

        a. Reliability
        b. Curiosity
        c. Empathy
        d. Creativity

9. The route to success is based on:

        a. Following proven methods
        b. Experimentation
        c. An inspiring vision
        d. Taking action

10. I'm most interested in:

        a. Meeting my responsibilities
        b. Solving problems
        c. Uncovering possibilities
        d. Making things work

Total the number of times you choose each letter				
a =	b =	c =	d =	Total = 10
Guardian Style	Rational Style	Idealist Style	Artisan Style	

As you probably guessed, the highest number will indicate the style that you are most likely to use.

So what do you do with this information?

Knowing your style is not meant to put you in a box. Nor does it say, "This is how you always behave or should behave." It's a starting place for you to think about how you communicate and a framework for noticing other people's styles. Adapting your own style to include elements from the other person's style will help you be better understood.

For example, Idealists and Rationals naturally see the big picture and focus on the future. When they talk to Artisans or Guardians, it will help if they focus on practical evidence that their ideas will work in the here and now. Guardians and Rationals, who naturally focus on facts and logic, are wise to include language that recognizes feelings and excitement when talking to an Idealist or Artisan. Idealists who can support their inspiring visions with practical arguments based in fact will be better heard and understood by the other styles.

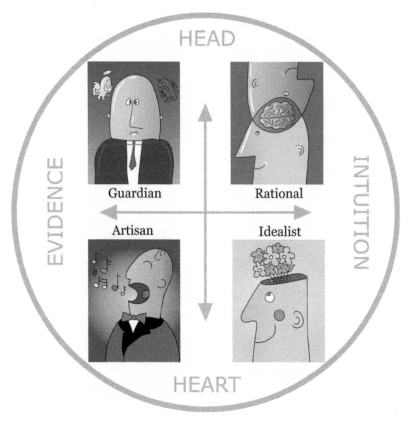

Guardians and Rationals tend to be ruled by their heads, while Artisans and Idealists listen to their hearts. Rationals and Idealists are comfortable using their intuition to make decisions. Artisans and Guardians want external evidence.

Think about the people you deal with every day. Each of them will likely use one style more than others, based on his or her ways of experiencing the world and making decisions. What drives each of them? Which style is most like each?

"We need to see our differences as something other than flaws." – David Keirsey

The Guardian Style At A Glance

People who operate in the Guardian style are driven by security and stability. They trust traditional ways of doing things, value credentials, trust authority and pride themselves on being reliable and hard working. They like to fit into the group and abide by the norms.

Stress pattern: They are stressed out by disloyalty and being "out of the loop." When that happens, they react by complaining and may even become ill.

Often heard to say: "If it's not broken, don't fix it."

Communicating with a Guardian: Use concrete facts and data and examples drawn from the real world. Look for ways your idea contributes to continuity. Show a reliable process at work. If you are communicating about a change, show how the change preserves something important. In choosing your language, think of process and reliability. On a personal level, state your appreciation for the Guardian's work and make them feel part of the group.

The Rational Style At A Glance

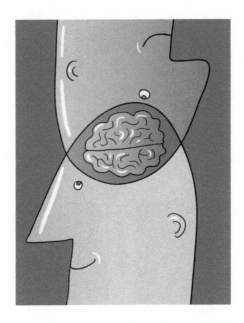

People who operate in the Rational style are driven by knowledge, competence and mastery. They value self-control and intellect. They like to solve problems. They trust logic and rely on their knowledge and theoretical understanding. They are achievement oriented, skeptical and strategic.

Stress pattern: Feeling powerless stresses them out, as do ignorance and incompetence. When stressed, they may obsess, engage in disaster scenarios, and don't think well.

Often heard to say: "There must be a better way to do this."

Communicating with a Rational: Use facts and ideas that draw the "big picture." Explain the logic behind your idea and show the brilliance of the project or solution. Show what problems your idea solves and how it solves them. Show the future value of your idea. In choosing your words, think of problems and solutions. On a personal level, affirm their competence and knowledge.

The Idealist Style At A Glance

People who operate in the Idealist style are driven by identity and self-awareness. They're enthusiastic, often inspiring. They pride themselves on compassion and empathy and value relationships. Authenticity is important to them. They seek meaning and purpose in their lives. They dream of attaining wisdom.

Stress pattern: They are stressed out by inauthenticity, lack of integrity, and betrayal; when stressed, they may withdraw or simply "play the role" rather than engage fully.

Often heard to say: "What will this mean for the people?"

Communicating with an Idealist: Paint a vision for the future that shows the "big picture." Use expressive language that recognizes feelings. If you're communicating about change, show concern for the impact on people. In choosing your words, think of a mission or quest. On a personal level, provide feedback and affirmation that you appreciate this person's work. You almost can't overdo this with Idealists.

The Artisan Style At A Glance

People who operate in the Artisan style are driven by sensations and spontaneity. They are practical, realistic and have a "can do" approach to things. They value action and are good trouble-shooters. They are creative; they love to improvise and use available resources to get things done.

Stress pattern: Usually fun-loving, they are stressed by limits and constraints, dull routine, and things that prevent them from acting. When stressed, they can become reckless, taking unnecessary risks, and seek retaliation.

Often heard to say: "Here's something that just might work."

Communicating with an Artisan: Use practical facts and concrete details and focus in the present. Avoid theoretical explanations and focus on what can be done. Show how your idea is innovative or nifty and will have impact. In choosing your words, think about emphasizing novelty. On a personal level, recognize their ingenuity and resourcefulness.

The ideas in this booklet were inspired by ideas from Carl Jung, Catherine Briggs and Isabel Briggs Meyers, and David Keirsey. For a more detailed assessment based on validated research, we recommend taking the Myers-Briggs Type Inventory (MBTI) or Keirsey Temperament Sorter.

APPENDIX

Learn More

VISIT THE **TALK TO ME** WEBSITE http://talktomebook.com where you'll find work sheets and other materials related to the information in this book.

BOOKS

Buckingham, Marcus and Don Clifton. *Now Discover Your Strengths*. New York: Free Press: 2001.

Cross, Jay. *Informal Learning: Rediscovering the Natural Pathways that Inspire Learning and Performance*. San Francisco: Pfeiffer, 2007.

D'Aprix, Roger. *Communication in the 21st Century: The Challenges, The Needs and the Answers*. San Francisco: International Association of Business Communicators, 2001.

Gladwell, Malcolm. *Blink, The Power of Thinking Without Thinking*. New York: Little Brown, 2005.

Goldsmith, Marshall. *What Got You Here Won't Get You There, How Successful People Become More Successful*. New York: Hyperion, 2007.

Goleman, Daniel, Richard Boyatzis and Annie McKie. *Primal Leadership: Learning to Lead with Emotional Intelligence*. Boston: Harvard, 2002.

Goleman, Daniel. *Social Intelligence: The New Science of Human Relationships*. New York: Bantam, 2006.

Kayser, Ken. *Mining Group Gold: How to Cash In on the Collaborative Brain Power of a Team for Innovation and Results.* New York: McGraw-Hill, 2011.

Keirsey, David. *Please Understand Me II: Temperament, Character, Intelligence.* New York: Prometheus Nemesis Book Company, 1996.

Patterson, Kerry. Joseph Grenney, Ron McMillan, and Al Switzler, *Crucial Conversations: Tools for Talking when Stakes are High.* New York: McGraw-Hill, 2002.

Pink, Dan. *Drive: The Surprising Truth About What Motivates Us.* New York: Penguin, 2009.

Pink, Dan. *A Whole New Mind, Why Right-Brainers Will Rule the Future.* New York: Penguin, 2006.

Rock, David. *Quiet Leadership: Six Steps To Transforming Performance at Work.* New York: HarperCollins, 2006.

Rock, David. *Your Brain At Work: Strategies for Overcoming Distraction, Regaining Focus, and Working Smarter All Day Long.* New York: HarperCollins, 2009.

Scott, Susan. *Fierce Conversations: Achieving Success at Work and in Life One Conversation at a Time.* New York: The Berkley Publishing Group, 2004.

Seligman, Martin. *Learned Optimism: How to Change Your Mind and Your Life.* New York: Pocket Books, 2006.

Stone, Douglas, Bruce Patton, and Sheila Hee., *Difficult Conversations: How to Discuss What Matters Most.* London: Penguin Books, 2000

Watkins, Jane Magruder and Bernard J. Mohr. *Appreciative Inquiry: Change at the Speed of Imagination.* San Francisco: Jossey-Bass/Pfeiffer, 2001.

Zander, Benjamin and Rosamond Stone Zander. *The Art Of Possibility, Transforming Professional and Personal Life.* New York: Penguin, 2002

USEFUL ARTICLES

David Rock. SCARF: A Brain-based Model for Collaborating with and Influencing Others (first published in the Neuroleadership Journal). http://www.your-brain-at-work.com/files/NLJ_SCARFUS.pdf March 31, 2012

Macomber, Hal. *Securing Reliable Promises on Projects: A Guide to Developing a New Practice.* Reforming Project Management http://www.reformingprojectmanagement.com/docs/securing-reliable-promises-on-projects.pdf March 31, 2012

Wise men talk because they have something to say, fools because they have to say something. – Plato

5

Katy's Best Biscotti Recipe

We suspect Katy opened The Coffee Grounds as an excuse to bake, serve and eat biscotti. These crisp, dense Italian biscuits come in many flavors and are baked twice, so they're almost rock-hard. That makes them perfect for dunking in frothy beverages such as cappuccino and hot chocolate. This is Katy's favorite recipe, adapted and tested by the author.

Chocolate Chaos (introduced in Chapter Four)
Makes about 20 biscuits | preparation – 10 minutes | baking/waiting/baking again – 1 hr. 15 min.
Oven 350° F (180° C) then 325° F (160° C)

CHOCOLATE CHAOS BISCOTTI

1 cup slivered almonds
1/4 cup unsalted butter
2/3 cup packed brown sugar
1 large egg
1/4 cup semi-sweet chocolate chips
1/4 cup milk chocolate chips
1/4 cup white chocolate chips
1 1/4 cups all-purpose flour

1. Toss almonds in a dry frying pan and toast over medium heat till browned. Let cool.

2. Cream butter and sugar. You can beat by hand or use an electric mixer.

3. Add egg and beat till light.

4. Add almonds and chocolate chips.

5. Blend in flour and mix well. The dough will be sticky.

5. Line baking tray with parchment (or silicon baking mats).

7. Shape dough into a long, flat log, about 3-in. (7.5 cm.) wide.

8. Bake log at 350° F (180° C) for 25 minutes.

9. Remove from oven and let cool for 30 minutes.

10. Cut the log into 1/2-inch (1 cm.) slices.

11. Distribute the slices on the baking tray.

12. Bake at 325° F (160° C) for 20 minutes.

In theory, these hard, dry biscuits will keep in an airtight container for three weeks. We have not seen evidence of this. Ours disappear very quickly.

6

About the Author

Sue is dedicated to improving the world, one conversation at a time. She believes real conversation is the most powerful tool we will ever use. "Don't send a letter when talking is better," has been her philosophy since she was a corporate communications rookie, writing newsletters for executives. She often persuaded them to abandon the print piece and, instead, prepared them to talk to people.

As a writer and trainer, Sue brings coaching skills and a lifelong study of interpersonal communication to her experience in senior management, corporate training and communication consulting.

Midway through a master's degree, she concluded – to her dismay – that the profession she had practiced for many years and was now studying was overlooking the most important aspect of communication at work – how people talk to each other. She set out to do something about that, establishing *It's Understood Communication* to work at the intersection of business and communication to help create better workplaces.

The learning journey continued at The Graduate School of Coaching, Six Seconds EQ, Psychometrics Canada, and Results Coaching/Neuroleadership Group.

She has a BA (Sociology/Psychology) from Bishop's University and an MBA (Communication Management) from Royal Roads University. She has earned professional accreditation by the Institute of Canadian Bankers (ICB), the International Association of Coaching (IAC) and the International Association of Business Communicators (IABC). She is a past regional chair of IABC, where she continues to volunteer.

Sue began her communication career in journalism, working at the Canadian Broadcasting Corporation, *The Edmonton Journal,* and *The London Free Press.* She then spent 10 years as an internal communications specialist in Canada's financial services giants, TD/Canada Trust and BMO/Bank of Montreal. She worked with communication agencies and nonprofits in Bermuda, where she lived for nine years. Now, she's based in Waterloo, Ontario, Canada where she can be reached through her web site, http://itsunderstood.com. She tweets as @itsunderstood.

CPSIA information can be obtained
at www.ICGtesting.com
Printed in the USA
BVHW03s1433150218
508094BV00003B/315/P